£2

IN THE HIGHLANDS AND ISLANDS

By the same author

THE SWISS ARMY

IN THE
HIGHLANDS AND ISLANDS

JOHN McPHEE

faber and faber
LONDON · BOSTON

This collection first published in 1986 by
Faber and Faber Limited
3 Queen Square London WC1N 3AU

Photoset by Parker Typesetting Service, Leicester
Printed in Great Britain by
Redwood Burn Ltd
Trowbridge, Wiltshire
All rights reserved

The Crofter and the Laird was published by
Farrar, Straus and Giroux, New York, in 1970
and originally appeared in *The New Yorker* in 1969.
'Josie's Well', 'Pieces of the Frame' and 'From Birnam
Wood to Dunsinane' were published by Farrar, Straus and
Giroux, New York, in 1975 as part of the collection
Pieces of the Frame, published simultaneously in Canada by
McGraw-Hill Ryerson Limited, Toronto.
These three stories originally appeared in *Holiday*, 1970,
The Atlantic, 1970, and *The New Yorker*, 1970, respectively.

British Library Cataloguing in Publication Data

McPhee, John
In the Highlands and islands.
1. Highlands (Scotland) — Description
and travel
I. Title
914.11'104858   QA880.H7

ISBN 0–571–14599–X

Contents

The Crofter and the Laird   *page* 1

Josie's Well   108

Pieces of the Frame   120

From Birnam Wood to Dunsinane   137

The Crofter and the Laird

The Scottish clan that I belong to – or would belong to if it were now anything more than a sentimental myth – was broken a great many generations ago by a party of MacDonalds, who hunted down the last chief of my clan, captured him, refused him mercy, saying that a man who had never shown mercy should not ask for it, tied him to a standing stone, and shot him. The standing stone was in a place called Balaromin Mor, on Colonsay, a small island in the open Atlantic, twenty-five miles west of the Scottish mainland. The event was not the first of its kind there, and in a sense the MacDonalds were only completing what had been begun in an earlier era, when a party of MacLeans landed on Colonsay, hunted down another chief of the native clan, and trapped him in a long and narrow cave. The cave had an entrance at each end. Somewhere between the entrances, there was an opening in the ceiling. The chief ran back and forth, apparently wondering which exit might be the safest, and at one moment he paused to contemplate the opening overhead. A MacLean who had been waiting for him to do just that killed him with an arrow from above. Certain other islands are prominently visible from Colonsay when the air is clear. The weather changes so abruptly there – closing in, lifting, closing in again – that all in an hour wind-driven rain may be followed by calm and hazy sunshine, which may then be lost in heavy mists that soon disappear into open skies

1

over dark-blue seas. When the ocean is blue, the air is as pure as a lens, and the other islands seem imminent and almost encroaching, although they are at least ten or fifteen miles away – Mull, for example, Scarba, Islay, Jura, the Isles of the Sea. In summer, toward midnight, the sun falls behind Tiree, thirty-five miles to the north-west, and Tiree becomes suddenly visible, back-lighted, apparently suspended in the air. In the time of the clans, Mull and Tiree, northern Jura, Scarba, and the Isles of the Sea were islands of the Clan MacLean. They form a semicircle around Colonsay to the north and east. Islay and lower Jura, which extend the semicircle to the south of Colonsay, were islands of the Clan Donald. Each of these clans, the MacLeans and the MacDonalds, had enormous territories of island and mainland to its name, but each apparently felt a need for seventeen additional square miles – this one small break in the Atlantic horizon, the sole territory of a small clan, never more than a few hundred people, whose title to the island had come by immemorial occupation. A clan without land was a clan broken. What the MacLeans had once failed to secure, the MacDonalds took and held.

In dependence on the MacDonalds and the various lairds who have followed them, many of the original clansmen remained on Colonsay. Others, beginning what would be a long-continuing but always voluntary emigration to the mainland, went to Lochaber, in the Great Glen, below Ben Nevis, and there entered into a kind of vassalage under the Cameron of Lochiel. On Culloden Moor many of them died with the Camerons, and modern books that deal with the clans and all the Highland souvenirs (tartans, plaids, kilts, claymores) will say that the Colonsay clansmen 'charged desperately' there. But everyone was desperate at Culloden, for all the clans were broken there – annihilated by English armies – and the seven-hundred-year era of regional government by the clan system was ended forever. Shortly afterward, acts of Parliament disarmed the clans, prohibited the wearing of tartan cloth (the ban was effective for nearly forty years), and permanently removed from all clans their hereditary jurisdictions. From that day on, now more than two hundred years, the clans have survived only in the air, and all their setts and badges and bearings are pure nostalgia.

There was a toast among the clans when they banqueted. A clansman would rise, lift a cup, and say, 'To the land of the bens and the glens!' And up from the food the faces would move, and every man would roar out, 'To the land of the bens and the glens!' The bens and the glens were the whole world, the clan world, and not even Sir Walter Scott could exaggerate the romantic beauty of that lake and mountain country penetrated by fjords that came in from seas that were starred with islands. But, unfortunately, by the time of Walter Scott all that was left up there was the scenery. The clans were gone, and so were the clansmen. The glens were empty, and it was possible in countless places to stand on high ground and look out over an area where, say, ten thousand people had lived and where the only inhabitants now were thirty or forty shepherds. After Culloden, the surviving chiefs became landowners – lairds – in the modern sense. The clan ideas of familial possession and patriarchal responsibility fell away. The clansmen became tenants, and the chiefs, in the course of things, sold them out. The 'dreamy, improvident Highlanders', as one Scottish historian has called them, all but gave away their patrimony to men from the Lowlands and from England. Before long, absentee owners heavily outnumbered resident lairds. To the new lairds it was clear enough that their lands were more profitable under sheep than under people, and so the people had to go. A small-farm society had evolved in the glens, and in the islands as well. The clansmen had shifted their concentration from war to agriculture, and life was agreeable enough, albeit primitive, in the small villages, with patches of ground under each man's tillage, cattle on the common grazing, and milk, vegetables, cheese, and meat on the table. The houses of the clansmen were called black houses, because peat was burned in them in open fires on hearthstones set in the middle of dirt floors, and the peat smoke seeped out through various holes in the thatch above after coating the interior of the house with smudge. Cattle and horses lived in the houses, too, or in adjacent byres. The animals often used the same entrance the people used. Windows were not glazed. When cold winds were blowing, the windows were stuffed with sod. In the late eighteenth and early nineteenth centuries, the glens were virtually swept clean of these people – the residue of the clans – and the lairds, in removing them, apparently felt no moral encumbrances. Their factors – general agents, business managers, collectors of rent – went around to the black houses and gave the people notice of their evictions, and at the appointed times the walls of the houses were pulled down and the thatch and the wooden beams were destroyed by flame. Families sat on hillsides, often in snow or rain, and watched their homes burn out. For seven hundred years, torches had called the clans together in time of need, and now torches cleared the glens. The people leaving sometimes had to drain blood from their cattle and drink it in order to survive.

From the perspective of the late twentieth century, there seems to be only one possible view of the Highland clearances, as they are called, but contemporary writers often showed different attitudes. Harriet Beecher Stowe went to Scotland and returned to the United States to write something called *Sunny Memories of Foreign Lands*, in which she defended what the lairds were doing. And

Robert Chambers, in his *Picture of Scotland*, published in 1827, wrote, 'The landlords have very properly done all they could to substitute a population of sheep for innumerable hordes of useless human beings, who formerly vegetated upon a soil that seemed barren of everything else.' The sheep were brought in by hundreds of thousands, and to some of the retreating population they became known as 'the lairds' four-footed clansmen'. Meanwhile, the clansmen themselves had three principal choices. They could move to the edge of the sea, which they hated, and live on fish, which most of them also hated. They could move to the Lowlands. Or they could emigrate to other continents. Into the middle of this tide went many of the original clansmen of Colonsay, some early, some later on, some after long stays on the mainland, others more directly from the island, some settling in the Lowlands, notably in Renfrewshire, others going to Australia, Canada, or the United States. Of those who left the Highlands as a result of the clearances, my own particular forebears were among the last. When my great-grandfather married a Lowland girl, in West Lothian, in 1858, he was in the middle of what proved to be a brief stopover between the bens and the glens and Ohio. He worked in a West Lothian coal mine, and the life underground apparently inspired him to keep moving. Serfdom in Scottish coal mines had been abolished in 1799, but Scottish miners of the mid-nineteenth century might as well have been serfs. They worked regular shifts of fifteen hours and sometimes finished their week with a twenty-four-hour day. Six-year-old girls in the mines did work that later, in times of relative enlightenment, was turned over to ponies. Wages were higher and hours a little shorter for mine work in the Mahoning Valley of Ohio, and my great-grandfather decided, in the early eighteen-sixties, to go there. The United States was torn up with civil war, and it is interesting to me but not surprising that that did not change his mind. He went into the Ohio mines, and stayed there, and died in 1907. He has about a hundred and thirty descendants who have sprayed out into the American milieu, and they have included railroad engineers, railroad guards, brakemen, firemen, steelworkers, teachers, football coaches, a chemist, a chemical engineer, a policeman, a grocer, salesmen, doctors, lawyers, druggists, janitors, and postmen. His son Angus, my grandfather, was a heater in a steel mill. He got the ingots white-hot and ready for the roller. He ate his lunch out of a metal box and never developed much loyalty to the steel company, possibly because his immediate superior was his brother-in-law. 'Oh, God damn it, Angus, if it weren't for my sister, I'd fire you,' the brother-in-law said once, and my grandfather said, 'John, if it weren't for your sister, I wouldn't have to work.' On New Year's Eve – or, rather, in the first hours of the new year – these Scotsmen in Ohio always went around to one another's houses, following the Highland custom of first-footing. The first foot to cross a threshold in a new year will bring untold beneficence if it is an acceptable foot. It has to be the foot of a dark-haired person. If the first-footing is done by a fair-haired person, that is all right as long as a lump of coal or some other dark object is thrown across the threshold first. My father remembers all this from his youth, but he raised his own family in Princeton, New Jersey, and there were no first-footings there.

It has always seemed extraordinary to me how the name of the island, Colonsay, seems to hang suspended in the minds not only of my immediate relatives but also of collateral clansmen in scattered parts of the United States and Canada, whose stories – from island to mainland to emigration – are essentially the same, and whose historical remoteness from Colonsay is comparable. Just the name of the island seems to set off in virtually all these people, who now live anywhere between the oceans, some sort of atavistic vibration, and all they really have in common is the panoptic glaze that will appear in their eyes at the mention of the word 'Colonsay'. Given the combined efforts of the MacLeans, the MacDonalds, and the sheep farmers of Lochaber, it is hard to imagine a clan more broken and rebroken and dispersed than this one, but the name of its aboriginal island still apparently brings a sense of true north to all these conductors, brakemen, lawyers, salesmen, and football coaches. Not long ago, it occurred to me that although all my clansmen in America had talked for so long about Colonsay, as far as I knew none of them had ever been there. For that matter, all that I knew about it was that it was one of the Hebrides, in the islands of Argyll. As soon as I could, I took my wife and our four young daughters and went to live for a while on Colonsay.

It was a custom within clans that clansmen sometimes brought up one another's children. In fact, the essential idea of the clan – a political unit based on blood and with its territory held not by the chief but by the clan as a whole – was often expressed in the handing over of the infant son of a chief to an ordinary clansman for upbringing. 'Kindred to forty degrees, fosterage to a hundred' was an expression among the clans – also, 'Affectionate to a man is a friend, but a foster brother is as the life blood of his heart'. Bonds of friendship between two clans were occasionally emphasized in the same way. It happened once that the chief of Colonsay and his good friend the Macneil of Barra found that their wives were both pregnant, and, in what must have been a scene of backslapping conviviality, the two men decided not only to have their new children raised on each other's island but to have them born on each other's island as well. Barra is seventy-five miles from Colonsay, over open sea, beyond Tiree. As his wife's time approached, the Macneil was apparently in no hurry to make the trip. The season was midwinter, but anxiety was not his predominant characteristic. His island was small, and its satellite islands – among them Mingulay, Vatersay, Eriskay – were little more than rocks, but he was *the* Macneil, the sort of man that was once called mighty. In the evenings after dinner, the Macneil would go out onto the battlements of his sea-bound Kisimul Castle, wipe his lips, sound a trumpet, and shout into the Atlantic winds, 'Hear, O ye people! And listen, O ye nations! The Macneil of Barra has eaten! The princes of the earth may now dine!' The Macneil's wife, at the end of her pregnancy, sailed for Colonsay in an open boat. In the middle of the trip, the boat – pitching, tossing – ran into a violent snowstorm. Mrs Macneil went into labour, and while the snow was still falling her child, a boy, was born. A cow was on board, and to save the baby and its mother from death by exposure the crew killed the cow, eviscerated her, and placed the mother and the child inside the warm carcass. The baby was named John, and all his life he was known as John of the Ocean. In his youth, he decided that he loved Colonsay too much to leave it. His counterpart, meanwhile, born on Barra, moved to Colonsay at an age that is now unknown and became chief. The foster brothers apparently developed a strong friendship, and the young chief of Colonsay gave John of the Ocean honoured status and a house, and although the wives of the two turned out to be jealous and inimical shrews, John of the Ocean remained on Colonsay all his life.

The line of Macneils that John introduced there is on the island still, and one of these is the crofter Donald McNeill, who on his maternal side is a descendant of Colonsay's original clan. His croft is on the western side of Colonsay, and from his house and his steadings the ground rises in green leas as it extends out toward the water, sometimes rising so sharply that the crofter's sheep have cut terraced tracks in order to keep their feet as they graze. The grassland ends in cliffs three hundred feet above the sea. The cliff face is slightly concave. In its clefts and on its ledges live thousands of kittiwakes, guillemots, razorbills, and fulmars, and above them, on the upper lip of the escarpment, great hunks of sod grow cantilevered out over the empty space above the waves. The crofter's cattle graze right up to the cliff edge, and once every two or three years a cow will step on the wrong plot of sod and go spinning to its death where breakers crash on the rocks below. It is cheaper to get another cow than it would be to fence the whole impossible shoreline of the croft, but the loss is a severe one nonetheless. The croft has eighteen acres under tillage, a figure well within the maximum – forty-nine acres – that defines a croft and was established by the Crofters' Holdings Act of 1886, which resulted from the Highland clearances and was written to protect the small tenant farmer and give him tenure on the land he worked.

Donald McNeill's father, Gilbert McNeill, worked the same croft, and so did *his* father, Donald McNeill, and his father, Gilbert McNeill, and his father, Donald McNeill. In each of these generations were siblings who emigrated to the mainland or to America, and sometimes everybody in the family went except the one who stayed with the croft. Donald has one brother, and he is now a policeman in Dunbartonshire. Donald once had a calendar on his kitchen wall that showed, in irresistible colour, the mountain forests of British Columbia. It was Donald's wife – Margaret MacMillan MacArthur McNeill – who put the calendar there, and even before its time had run out she knew that her daydreams of British Columbia were aimless ones, because Donald would never leave Colonsay. He won't even go off the island for a holiday, let alone a lifetime. He goes to the mainland when he has to, ordinarily to sell animals, about once a year. His wife has seen the mainland very few times. For all the passing thoughts of western Canada she may once have had, she is quick to say that not seeing the Scottish mainland is no hardship on her. She is tall and fair-haired, and has sad blue eyes that can flash with sardonic humour. She also is a native of the island, and her affection for it seems to be even stronger than her husband's. The calendar picture is long since gone from the wall.

There are seventeen crofts on Colonsay and seven farms (a farm has more than forty-nine tillable acres), and a hundred and thirty-eight people, of two castes. About eighty are islanders, like the McNeills, and the rest are incomers. The incomers, for the most part, are people who were born on the mainland or on other islands or whose fathers or grandfathers were born on the mainland or on other islands. What constitutes an islander, apparently, is a familial history of unbroken residence on Colonsay for two or three hundred years. The islanders, for the most part, are crofters and farmers. The incomers are the doctor, the postman, the postmaster, the schoolteacher, the innkeeper, the storekeeper, the minister – the permanently unestablished establishment. Another incomer is the laird, who owns the island. He owns all the crofts, the farms, the store, the inn (thirty-seven beds) – everything but the tiny church and school properties and the pier, which was built by the Argyll County Council. The laird is not, however, actually a part of the Colonsay population, although he spends two or three months on the island in most years. He is in principle an absentee landlord. He is English and lives in Bath.

The laird inherited Colonsay from his father ten years ago, and is still identified in the speech of the people as the new laird. The old laird was a quiet and benevolent man who wanted more than anything else not to have to listen to grumbling tenants during his short vacations on the island, so he was liberal in the allowances that he made for improvements in the real estate. He once decided that several of the crofters' houses – thick-walled stone houses with two rooms and two lofts – were no longer habitable, so he built new and somewhat larger houses for them, and he left the old houses standing. Thus several Colonsay crofters, in a situation that may be unique in the Highlands, have two houses. Donald McNeill has two, one right next to the other. And when occasion arises, usually during the months of long daylight, he will move out of the newer house and sublet it – which is what he did for me and my family – meanwhile making his own family quite comfortable in the uninhabitable house next door in which he grew up, and in which, in 1925, as the first result of the marriage between the son of Donald McNeill and the daughter of Donald McPhee, he was born.

As a boy, Donald Gibbie – as he has always been called, because the name identifies him as Donald son of Gilbert – went to the common grazing each morning as soon as he got up, to locate and bring in the cows. Sometimes he was told to fetch a horse as well. First he found and then he followed the tracks of the animals, which he recognized individually, in the dew. The search and the return took as much as two hours, for the common grazing, which the McNeills shared with seven other crofters, was a little more than six hundred acres, and to find the animals Donald Gibbie often had to go to very high ground, near the summits of A' Bheinn Bhreac (the Speckled Peak) and Binnean Riabhach (the Brindled Pinnacle). These hills are only about four hundred feet high, but they are considerable hills nonetheless, since they rise almost straight from the ocean. Every day, also, Donald Gibbie took two pails and walked four hundred yards to a well for water. The language of the house was Gaelic and Gaelic only. He learned English in school, from a teacher who taught all levels from age five to fourteen, as the Colonsay teacher still does. He also learned to step to the side of the road, take off his cap, and bow his head when the laird went by in a gig driven by a coachman in a bowler hat. (Automobiles were not introduced to the island until 1947.) The house, with its stone walls and its slate roof, was of a design repeated on crofts throughout the Highlands. Covered by blankets woven from Colonsay wool, Donald and his younger brother slept on corn-chaff mattresses in the room loft, under the steeply peaked slate roof, and his mother and father slept in the other upstairs room, the kitchen loft. Below the room loft was 'the room', which took up half the house on the ground floor and was twelve feet by twelve. It was set apart for visitors, for first-footings, for wedding receptions, and for little else. The entire house had something like six hundred square feet of living space (less than the size of one floor of a New York brownstone), yet twenty-five per cent of it was set apart from daily use. Even today, Donald and his family do not really use 'the room', and it serves them as little more than an enormous storage closet. 'The room' was separated from the kitchen by a thick stone partition that contained a fireplace on each side. The kitchen was literally and completely the living room. It had a drop-leaf table, a long wooden seat near the fire, various chairs, settees. In the fireplace were a cast-iron cooking surface and a cast-iron oven. That is how the kitchen still looks. When Donald was twelve, he took over the milking of the cows. His mother used to make seventeen pounds of butter a week, in a plunger churn. It was also when he was twelve that he saw the mainland for the first time. His mother took him there for a tonsillectomy. When he was fourteen, he had to give up his education, because then, as now, a Colonsay child who wanted an education beyond the limits of the Colonsay school had to go to the mainland, finding room and board there in a hostel or with a mainland family, and since that cost more money than a crofter could afford, the only way to go was to take competitive examinations and qualify for a bursary from the Scottish Education Department. Donald Gibbie took the examinations but didn't qualify. The Second World War began, and, still scarcely in his teens, he was drafted into the coal mines of Fife and Kent. By the time he came home, he probably looked pretty much the way he does now – of middle height, with long, dark hair, dark eyes, high and prominent cheekbones, lips that seem to be permanently pursed and pensive, and a strong and tense frame.

He worked on one of the island farms for a while, and he became, as well, a lobsterman. He has long since given up being a lobsterman commercially, but he still knows the name and address of every Colonsay lobster. One day, after I had been telling him what I thought to be the truth – that there was no lobster on earth that was remotely similar or qualitatively comparable to the lobster of Maine – Donald Gibbie put on a pair of knee-length rubber boots, and, while the tide dropped, we walked the three miles from the croft to the outer shoals of the Ardskenish Peninsula, where the best lobsters are. The Ardskenish Peninsula juts a couple of thousand yards into the Atlantic in a southwesterly direction, and its low, fairly even ground is so unprotected that people who have been caught out there by strong northeasterly winter gales have sometimes had to crawl back against the wind, or they have simply stayed there lying flat, for hours if necessary, waiting for the wind to drop. A farmhouse, two storeys high, standing empty, projects upward incongruously from the middle of the peninsula. The sun was shining that day, the wind was gentle, and along the periphery of Ardskenish the low tide left clear pools among the skerries. Brown Atlantic seals and one grey seal dived from rocks as we splashed along through the tidal pools. The seals swam around offshore, heads up, watching us with what had at first been alarm and now seemed to be interest and irritation. Donald Gibbie obviously knew exactly where he was going. With light, athletic motions, he moved as fast as he could, impatiently, over great pompadours of seaweed and through rock basins filled with still water. Now and then he went in deeper than the tops of his boots, but he had cut holes over the toes to let the water spurt out. He had with him a piece of heavy wire, about a quarter inch in diameter and five feet long. It was bent somewhat like a shepherd's crook at one end. Finally, in one of the tidal pools, he stopped at a place where, under the water, a small cavern, perhaps a foot high, went far back under an overhanging ledge of rock. Donald took the wire and reached with it into the cavern, his body assuming something of the stance of a fencer. Slowly he moved the wire from side to side, working it around as much of the cavern interior as he could probe. After two minutes or so, he said, 'He's not there now.' We moved on, as before, in and out of water, over seaweed beds, until Donald Gibbie stopped at another cavern. That lobster was not there, either. Donald Gibbie remarked that perhaps the tide was not low enough for him to get into some of the best places,

and he was sorry about it, because he had thought the
tide would be several feet lower that day. The walk
home was beginning to look like a long one. Then, after
bending over in front of the third lobster house and
working the wire back and forth, he said, 'I've got one.'
For three or four minutes he slowly turned and agitated
the wire. He wasn't trying to hook the lobster, he
explained, he was just trying to anger it. Very slowly, he
began to draw out the wire, meanwhile shaking it
enough to preserve the interest of whatever might be on
the other end. My scepticism stayed with me right to the
last. I don't know what I expected to see come out of
there – perhaps a snapping turtle, or some pretentious
crayfish from the Cape of Good Hope, or possibly a
clawless Spanish *langosta*. But suddenly out into the sunlight – hanging on to the wire and snapping at it like a
fence cutter – came several pounds of glistening,
mottled, dark blue-green lobster, in shape and appearance identical to the most expensive creature in Penob-
scot Bay. Donald seemed a little surprised when I said
the resemblance was so close, but he believed me, and
was impressed. He had apparently been sceptical, too.

'When I fished lobsters, I used creels and went out
every day in a boat,' he said, 'I didn't have a boat big
enough to stand the winter weather. I never did it all the
year round. We baited the creels with saithe and mac-
kerel. I had a partner. The boat was mine. We worked
eighty creels. On our best days, we got sixty or seventy
lobsters. Ordinarily, we would get about thirty.' He had
the wire deep in another cavern, and soon he was
engaged in a patient fight with another lobster. When
we started home, we had three of them. I told Donald
that the smallest of the three would be worth somewhere
between ten and fifteen shillings, over the counter, in
Maine, and that the biggest one – the first caught –
would be worth well over a pound. He said that the

lobsters in our hands (he had wrapped their claws with string) were worth a great deal more than that, since they can bring as much as a pound per pound nowadays to the lobsterman himself, let alone the storied sums they command in the retail markets of London. In his own day, he had got only three shillings and sixpence per pound. He had shipped the lobsters, in boxes, to Oban, or sometimes direct to Billingsgate, in London. He had to keep them alive for as long as a month while he waited for suitable transport to the mainland. Of the proceeds, a share went to the boat, a share to the gear, and a share to each partner. Working from May to November, Donald made about fifteen pounds a week. Anything under nine inches long went back into the sea, as did any lobster with spawn. He said that he had given up lobster fishing in 1957, when his father turned eighty and decided to stop working the croft. Since then, Donald went on, no one on Colonsay has fished lobsters commercially. The people don't fish for much of anything else there, either. In fact, they give the impression that they have, if not an active distaste for the sea, at least a thoroughgoing indifference to it. There are no commercial fishermen in the population. Cut off out there in the ocean, the people of Colonsay lead rural, agrarian, landlocked lives, growing their roots and vegetables and looking after their poultry and livestock, meanwhile turning their backs to the water whenever possible and in summer ignoring the island's splendid beaches. They eat fish rarely. Some years ago, the postmaster bought a deep freeze, in which he keeps a stock of frozen foods for sale. When fish *is* eaten on Colonsay. the freezer is where it comes from. The brand is Birdseye. For an islander of Colonsay, it was a most unusual and in a sense original thing that Donald Gibbie did when, for ten years, he worked at taking lobsters from the sea.

With our wives, we ate the three lobsters from Ardskenish after boiling them in sea water for twenty minutes, cracking them, and dipping the meat in drawn butter. The McNeills, who had tasted lobster only in bits with other foods, were interested in trying the New England method. However, I think both of them were appalled to see the equivalent of six or seven pounds sterling just vanish from the table after a bath in butter, but they said they found the lobsters delicious – as did my wife and I. The claw meat was a little sweeter than the claw meat of a Maine lobster. The rest was undifferentiable from its American counterpart. On the table as well was pure Highland malt whisky from Speyside, and it was just right with the Scottish lobster.

Given the view that most of the islanders seem to take of the sea, it is not surprising that Donald Gibbie barely knows how to swim. During the war, when he was working in the mines in Fife, he once went to a public swimming pool in Dunfermline, and while he was paddling around there he somehow caught his toe below a handrail and nearly drowned. He says that that put him off swimming forever. In a boat, though, he is unafraid of the ocean. He has had any number of small boats, and in them he has never hesitated to make long voyages, usually alone, to explore other islands, and he will even flirt with the Strait of Corryvreckan, eighteen miles east of Colonsay. Corryvreckan is a whirlpool celebrated in the history and legends of the Hebrides. Its spectral sucking and hissing can be heard from great distances over the water, and it has swallowed bigger boats than Donald Gibbie's. I once asked him what he would do if wind or wave ever separated him from his boat on one of his explorations, and he said, with an explosive laugh, 'Well, I guess I'd drown.'

Donald's experience with boats on the sea derives from something more than lobster fishing. He also worked for many years as a ferryman for MacBrayne's, the company that operates the mail boat to Colonsay. The mail boat calls three times a week, and the voyage from the mainland takes five hours. The island is absolutely dependent on the little steamer, the Lochiel, but until very recently, when the Argyll County Council built the Colonsay pier, the Lochiel had no place to tie up. It used to drop anchor some distance offshore, and a small boat, skippered by Donald Gibbie, would go out to pick up and deliver mail, passengers, and cargo. Frequently the ocean was so violent that the Lochiel would heave to for a while and wait; then, if it became clear that the ferry had no chance of surviving an attempt to make the connection, the Lochiel would go back to the mainland. When this happened, a small crowd of disappointed islanders and incomers anxious to receive or send goods, and inn guests due home from their island vacations, would abuse Donald Gibbie, since most of them had even less regard for the sea than he did. 'When inn guests were particularly arrogant,' he told me, 'I used to take them out a short distance, until they were thoroughly shaken up and soaking wet. They were happy enough to return to shore.' These ferries were not impressive vessels, probably no more so than the boat in which Mrs Macneil and her infant son John of the Ocean arrived from Barra. When Donald started with MacBrayne's, in the late nineteen-forties, as assistant ferryman, he learned some of his seamanship on a ferry he describes as 'a thirty-footer with an old Kelvin poppet fifteen-horse petrol paraffin engine – just to get near it, you had to have your wits about you'. But he never lost any cargo, not so much as a pipe cleaner, in seventeen years of ferrying people, cattle, sheep, mail, automobiles, and sometimes extraordinarily bulky cargo.

There was one aspect of all this that forced him

literally into the sea. Cattle, like autos, were swung over the ferry in slings depending from a small crane, then were lowered to the deck. The slings were placed under the bellies of the animals, and their legs hung down on either side. Donald stood in his boat and waited for each cow as she swung out over his head. It is not hard to envision how frightened a cow might be, hanging in a sling from a crane over a boat that was pitching and rolling at the edge of an apparently limitless expanse of rolling water. In two cases out of three, the tails of the cattle would rise and yesterday's cud would drop on Donald Gibbie. 'You just had to forget that they had an opening at the other end,' he told me. There was no going home for a bath after one of these cattle trips. There was nothing to do but jump into the sea beside the boat – in winter, often enough, in the almost total darkness of the mornings. Now, in the course of things, he has become the pier master, responsible for the operations of a long platform of white concrete that reaches out to deep water and from which cattle can walk onto the Lochiel. After our own voyage to Colonsay, over green and foaming waters in a wind that made tears run down our cheeks, the first person we saw was Donald Gibbie, standing there on his pier in the lee of Cnoc na Faire Mor (Big Lookout Hill), in his Wellington boots, his dungarees, his heavy grey pullover, and his brown-and-tan knitted cap, with his hands clasped behind his back, a frown on his face, and a look of felt responsibility in his eyes.

A few nights ago, when the McNeills asked us to come over to their house for a wee dram by the fire, I found myself telling them about American weddings and any number of peculiar rituals that sometimes complement the basic rites. Donald seemed particularly amused to learn that a few hours after my wife and I were married, in 1957, I had been surrounded by a cordon of friends – overmuscled, post-adolescent males with flaring nostrils – and, after a valiant struggle, had been pinned shirtless to the floor of an upstairs room at something called the Woman's Club of Ridgewood. There, despite continued resistance on my part, a set of messages – not in code – was written all over my chest, back, and shoulders in four shades of lipstick.

The McNeills responded to my story with one of their own. On the evening before a Colonsay wedding, they told me, all the chickens to be used in the next day's wedding feast are plucked in the bride's house by the friends and families of the betrothed, and the feathers are piled high in the middle of the room. The size of the pile is determined by the number of expected guests, and in their case the daughter of a crofter was about to marry the son of another crofter, and nearly every islander of Colonsay was related to one of the two families, so the pile of feathers was enormous. After the last chicken had been plucked, Donald stripped to the waist and prepared to do battle – as tradition required – against all the other men of roughly his age, with the hill of feathers as the battleground. Donald put up a good fight but was soon overwhelmed and, struggling violently, was pinned down by four others and all but buried in the feathers. He held his breath as long as he could, but finally he could hold it no longer, and inhaled. He said that he took in two lungfuls of pinfeathers and very nearly died right there. He came up purple, rapidly fading to grey – hacking, heaving, unable to find new breath. But enough oxygen finally got through the pinfeathers, and he was on his feet when he was married. The year was 1957.

That was also the year when Gilbert McNeill, who has since died, stopped working the croft and turned it over to his son. A true crofter, Donald has told me, works only part time on his croft, and turns to other resources to round out his income. For this reason, Donald puts in only about seventy hours a week working on the croft. He grows beef and mutton, and he has ninety breeding ewes and seven breeding cows. The laird's bull is available, at one pound sterling per visit. To feed his animals, Donald grows oats, turnips, hay, and potatoes. The family eats the potatoes, too, and if there is a surplus it is sold. The croft has ten or twelve chickens, mainly for eggs and rarely for the pot. One of the breeding cows doubles as a milk cow, so the McNeills make their own butter and their own crowdy (a form of cheese). Assessors for Her Majesty's Government have decided that the food the croft produces for the McNeills' own table is worth sixty pounds sterling a year, and Donald pays tax on that figure as income. He and Margaret also collect winkles, limpets, lobsters, clams, and mussels from the shore. They even go fishing once in a while. They eat rabbits, too. ('I remember when there was very little bought meat coming into any house on the island. Everyone ate rabbit, but for some time now the myxomatosis has put people off.') Deep in rabbit burrows, shelducks lay their eggs, and the McNeills sometimes collect and eat the eggs. They also eat the eggs of eider ducks, oyster catchers, and gulls – and often enough they eat the eider ducks, too, and shelducks, mallards, and pheasants. The pheasant population of Colonsay is probably ten times the human population, and one comes to recognize some of the pheasants individually, always foraging in pairs, models of fidelity, ageing gracefully together, sometimes all the way to the table. Once in a while, but rarely, Donald takes his shotgun and goes off to shoot a wild goat – never for sport but just for the meat. Goats were originally brought to Colonsay because it was known that they would assert territorial rights to the highest ground, thus keeping sheep away from the crags and contributing to their safety. The goats have long since gone completely wild, but their effect on the sheep is still the same. The McNeills also collect watercress from the streams, they make nettle soup, and they eat sea kale. But they do all this only in part to supplement their income. They do it, as well, because they get pleasure from it. Most of the food they eat comes either from grocers on the mainland who send out boxes of provisions on the Lochiel to fill private orders or from the small island store, whose sign, 'The Shop', painted in white letters on the side of the green building, is the only sign on Colonsay.

The McNeills collect and burn a great deal of driftwood to save coal. In winter, they go to the tidal pools of the Ardskenish Peninsula and gather winkles, which they can ship to the mainland and sell for two pounds a hundredweight. There are about seven thousand winkles in a hundredweight. On even a casual walk along the shore, Donald's eyes are always alert for a find of any sort. One day when we made a circuit of Ardskenish together, he came back with a boat hook, a large basket, a scrub brush, a stainless-steel bolt, a Norwegian plastic fishing float the size of a big balloon, and perhaps a dozen grapefruit-size aluminum floats of the type that a fishing boat uses to support a net. The floats bring two pounds a hundredweight. At home, the McNeills waste nothing. When their old steel teapot develops a leak, Donald plugs up the hole with a wood screw. I once picked up the teapot and looked inside. The points of fourteen screws intruded.

Margaret counts on the yield from winkle sales to give her the extra and special things she looks forward to having – a new rug, for example. She experienced a particularly bitter setback a couple of years ago when, after she had gathered winkles and shipped them to the mainland all through the winter, the firm to which the Lochiel had been delivering the winkles went bankrupt, and for the winter's work she collected nothing at all. There is some hazard, also, in shipping animals over the water, and none of this risk is assumed by the owners of the Lochiel. Before anyone can set foot or place goods on a MacBrayne's boat, a risk note must be signed freeing the company from all responsibility. After that, it's full steam ahead and hope for the best. A few years ago, the Lochiel, with a third mate at the helm, swung into West Loch Tarbert, near the mainland end of its route, lost the channel in a mist, crashed into a rock, lurched across the narrow sea loch and crashed into another rock, and then, with water pouring into her hold, made a desperate but unsuccessful attempt to get to the West Loch Tarbert pier, a few yards short of which she sank in twenty feet of water, stern in the air, bow down, with the surface of the sea loch lapping at the windows of the wheelhouse. Unfortunately, there were on the foredeck forty sheep that belonged to Donald Gibbie. They all drowned. The loss to him was two hundred and fifty pounds, the equivalent of the savings of four good years – a good year being one in which the net income of the croft, including the government subsidies he gets for his sheep and cattle, is about one hundred and fifty pounds.

For his work at the pier – about twenty hours a week – Donald gets four hundred and sixty-eight pounds a year from MacBrayne's. He is also the Colonsay constable, a job that takes almost no time and pays nothing, unless he can show loss of earning. And he is a coast-watcher for the Coast Guard. During big storms, he sits in a radio shack on Maol Chlibhe (the Bare Cliff) prepared to fire signal rockets and to call in compass bearings if he should see a ship in distress, and for this service he is paid thirty-three and six an hour. Adding all things together, the McNeills make the equivalent of about fifteen hundred dollars a year.

Not long after Donald took over the croft he began applying to the Crofting Commission for the right to fence off his part of the common grazing – his soamings on the hill. The Crofting Commission, which was set up soon after the first crofting act, has the jurisdiction over crofters that was once arbitrarily exercised by the lairds. To get permission to fence off his own part of the common grazing, a crofter has to show cause – and showing cause usually has to do with irresolvable difficulties with the crofters sharing the hill. But in Donald Gibbie's case I imagine that whatever cause he was able to show may have been less significant to him than the sense of independence he wanted to gain. At all events, he won out, and his croft and his grazing land are now integral and unshared, and he has run his fences far up the slopes of the Brindled Pinnacle. He has a hundred and forty-one acres in all, with seas breaking on two sides of it, high meadows, good water (from a deep well now), and good soil. His potatoes and oats win prizes in the island's annual competitions. And he also has his two houses, two byres, an implement shed (in the ruins of still another family house, a predecessor of the two now standing), a barn, and a stable. The doorways are painted red, and the walls of most of the buildings, low and compact, are of deep-grey Colonsay stone. For someone who loves this place as much as he obviously does, there could be no other in the world, and it is not hard to see why he would not leave it. His apparent affection for independence, however, rests uneasily on a paradox of his time. Protected and secured by the Crofters' Holdings Act, he has tenure on the land of his father and his grandfathers, and the rent he pays for all his land and buildings is only forty-five pounds a year – about a hundred and twenty dollars. If the croft were available to him to buy outright, he could not afford it. So his modified vassalage under the laird, though it may conflict with his hunger for personal freedom, is not something that he could readily give up. 'One feels that one is neither a proper crofter nor a proper landholder, sort of style' is the way he put it once. Parliament, concerned only that no repetition of the Highland clearances should ever occur, has preserved certain fragments of the Middle Ages in something like a gigantic block of clear plastic, and inside it is Donald Gibbie. The laird, for that matter, is in there, too, set, as is Donald Gibbie, within what has become the grand anachronism of the Highlands. 'Some crofters don't work their crofts,' Donald said. 'They have a cow, a few sheep. That is all. My father was always one for working the croft. When I took it over, I kept it going. It's not right to let the land be neglected. I'm quite happy here. I make out, so long as the shore's handy, and such like. But if you expect many things in life, crofting isn't the way to get them. Crofting cannot keep up with the times. Most people expect more than the bare necessities of living now. And crofting is not a livelihood. It's an existence.'

Between the two houses of the croft is a shed full of driftwood and coal. We collect driftwood frequently and pile it up in the shed, because we burn a great deal of it ourselves, particularly at night. The coal, which is brought out twice a year from the mainland in boats called puffers, costs twelve pounds a ton in its cheapest form – two-foot floes of it, like cakes of black ice. In the early mornings, I go outside and break up the coal with an axe. One bucketful is enough to give the stove in the kitchen a good start for the day. Ordinarily, the ashes are dead in the morning, because I am mediocre at preserving fire through the night. So I shake down the ashes, remove them, build a new fire, and take the ashes out to a rusted steel drum, where both families also throw the remains from the table. A cat and a rooster are always near the drum. If ashes go into it, they don't move. If garbage goes into it, the cat jumps in first and spends ten minutes inside. Then he jumps out, half grey with ash, and the rooster jumps in – thus the hierarchy of the croft.

The stove not only has a cooking surface and an oven but also heats a water tank and, often most important, emits some radiant heat in a house in which the temperature in the other rooms is usually around forty-five degrees at the beginning and end of the day. Colonsay has a consistent marine climate. The temperature rarely goes above sixty or below freezing at any time of the day or the year. The island is on the latitude of northern Labrador, Kodiak, and Novosibirsk, but the Gulf Stream peters out nearby, and a good thick Scottish pullover is all one needs here, perhaps two or more in winter. Each morning, until the stove has been going for a while no one else in my family will get up. Fortunately, we also have a bottled-gas hot plate, and I make tea for them – Melrose's Tartan Tips Tea – while they, wrapped in their blankets, females all, aged two to thirty-two, wait. Then they come into the kitchen and eat Jaffajuce grapefruit segments, toast and Chivers thick-cut marmalade, Scott's porridge or Kellogg's Rice Krispies, and cream from the McNeills' milk cow. After breakfast, the older two children go off with the McNeills' children to school.

The school day begins at nine-thirty – in a low, grey, roughcast building that has only one classroom. The hour is so late because of the distances that some of the children have to travel. Wee Ian, of Balnahard, whose age is twelve, has to drive a tractor three and a half miles to a point where the school bus can pick him up. The school bus is driven by Charlie McKinnon the Motor Hirer, whose route is limited by Colonsay's single paved road, which is little more than a loop through the centre of the island. The school's enrolment – twenty-three in all – is heavily unbalanced toward the earlier grades. Six children are in Primary 1, four in Primary 2. The teacher, Miss Walker, says, 'At the moment, there are so many wee tiny ones that I never seem to get beyond the reading, writing, and arithmetic.' There are no blackboards, because blackboards would be pointless in a schoolroom that contains children of ten ages. Miss Walker writes work on paper for each student, then moves from desk to desk. 'Please, Miss. Please, Miss, I am stuck,' someone calls out, and Miss Walker goes to that one to give help. 'I've been feeling my way to find the best way with this group,' Miss Walker has told me. 'I haven't found it yet. You've got to give quite a bit of attention to the wee-est ones at the moment. If I notice that someone isn't picking something up, I try to make time to go and help that person.' Now, after some weeks, she has said that she is pleased with the work of my two older daughters, because each of them – the one in Primary 4, the other in Primary 2 – is reading exactly at the Highland standard for her level, and one of them is right where she should be in counting, while the other is only slightly sub-par. I, for my part, am much impressed that the public-school system of Princeton, New Jersey, which once harboured me and is now, at home, responsible for the education of my children, seems to measure up to the level of an education on Colonsay.

At half past ten each morning, Miss Walker serves milk, with which the children eat biscuits they bring from home. She mixes the milk from powder that comes from a subdivision of the Argyll County Council, on the mainland. In their homes, Colonsay children drink milk of unsurpassable quality from cows on their crofts and farms, but at ten-thirty in the morning they drink powdered milk from Dunoon, to conform to regulations established to insure the good health of the children of Argyll. Then they run around outside – if the weather is all right – for a fifteen-minute period called 'the interval'. Back at their desks, they turn to the study of the English language, each writing in his own jotter, some of the young ones going through the *First Introductory English Workbook*.

Multiple choice: 'Instead of *large*, we could say (small) (big) (wee).'

Attention wanders. Discipline slips out of control. There is an event of insubordination. Miss Walker takes the offending boys into another room and straps them. Two boys once ran away from such a scene and fled overland. Miss Walker went after them in her automobile and brought them back to the strap.

Primary 4 is writing in its jotters. 'Saint Patrick of Ireland was born in Dumbarton, Scotland,' the children write. 'While he was still a boy, he moved to the side of the Solway Firth.' A little later, they write the story of the tanning of leather: 'Each skin is split into two pieces. The grain leather is the hair side. The suede leather is the flesh side.' Now they have a go at their McDougall's Semi-Vertical Copy Books. 'No gain without pain,' they write three times. 'Eisleben: the birthplace of Luther . . . Frankfurt: birthplace of Goethe . . . Kasanlik produces attar of roses.'

English is the language of the school, and the children hear Gaelic only at home. The school once used Gaelic in all its extracurricular aspects and English in the classroom. The children of incomers used to learn Gaelic within one year, but now they don't learn it at all, and this saddens Donald Gibbie. Unless someone comes into his home who speaks only English, Donald speaks Gaelic there throughout the day. So does Margaret. Their children understand, but answer in English. Donald thinks in Gaelic, even when he is speaking English. 'The

English of the isles is pure and good,' he told me. 'It's not pukka English, you know, but it's the King's English. The English of the isles is good because it is the second language and has been learned in school.'

It is, in fact, often said that the purest English spoken in the world is spoken in the Highlands. Tangled brogues and syntactical impurities sometimes misassociated with the Highlanders are the monopoly of the Lowland Scots. Idiomatic peculiarities in the Highlands are kept mainly in the Gaelic, the native tongue, and the acquired one, English, runs almost pure. A certain Gaelic tone and a certain Gaelic rhythm filter through into the English of the Highlanders, and the sounds of their voices carrying the words of the Sassenach are so beautiful that one almost resents having to hear the language anywhere else. In Gaelic, *Sasunn* is England. And a *Sasunnach* is an Englishman. The words are apparently never used as compliments. When Dr Johnson travelled through the islands, in the summer of 1773, he decided that both the islanders and their language were rude and barbaric, but he knew no Gaelic, and no judgement of his could have disturbed the self-assurance of the people of the Hebrides, who knew, as one Gaelic dictionary has put it, that 'in the islands of Argyll every word is pronounced just as Adam spoke it.'

The school day breaks at twenty minutes to one for dinner: stews, roast beef, roast pork, potatoes, vegetables, steam puddings, dumplings, fruit and custard — whatever is on the menu from Dunoon. At twenty minutes to one each day, all the schoolchildren in Argyll sit down to the same meal. A cook prepares it from supplies shipped out by the County Council. History follows, and geography, and a half hour of the Bible and another half hour of nature study. 'Or,' Miss Walker says, 'we just go out for a wee walk and see the wild flowers' — daisies, celandines, sea pinks, heath orchis, pheasant's-eyes, wild iris, whin, broom, meadow rue. When my daughters came home from school one day, one said to me, 'Daddy, we say prayers at school. What do you think of that? Did you do that when you were a little boy in school?'

'Yes, I think I did.'

'On Colonsay?'

'In Princeton.'

'In Princeton? You're kidding.'

'No, I'm telling you the truth. You're late today. What time is it?'

'It's just a wee bit past four.'

At home, I spend most of my time looking out of windows, and nothing changes the habit here. The window now – of a small room with a table-desk, a bed, a shelf, a cupboard – looks northwest across the cultivated acres of the croft, which are fenced to keep out the herds. Between the house and the fields, Donald Gibbie walks by with his cattle, knitted cap on his head, hands behind his back, moving fast, shouting angrily. His words are whips that pack the cattle together and keep them going. When Margaret brings the cattle in, they sometimes break and scatter in six directions, but they don't try that with Donald. They obviously feel his intensity, his acute sense of responsibility. Those things he eats are antacid tablets.

'Donald does his job one hundred per cent, whatever it is, come hell or high water, no matter whose toes he's going to tread on,' someone said to me one day. Few people on Colonsay – incomers or islanders – are shy of talking about one another.

'Donald makes up his own mind, and heaven and earth won't move him.'

'To live in this part of the world, you have to be a bit

of an individualist. People out here have strong minds and can't be led easily. He's quite a nice sort of man, is Donald Gibbie.'

'Och. He's a stubborn, bad-tempered devil. Cock of the walk. It is a wonder that he hasn't been shied off that pier.'

'Och. Everyone here likes to be the cock of the walk. They are all inclined to be like Donald Gibbie.'

'He's got a Highland sense of humour.'

'You could call him just a little bit dour, I think.'

'He has a nervous stomach. He worries. He loses his head.'

'Och. And *so* do you.'

'He goes white with temper. He raves at the boat passengers.'

'He's got a Highland sense of humour.'

'He's a very fair constable.'

'He always speaks well of people, I will say that.'

Donald ploughs one of the fields. His tractor is old and is so corroded by the salt air that it seems to be on the verge of ploughing itself in brown flakes into the soil. After the annual island ploughing contest, not long ago, Donald came home with three pounds ten shillings in prize money, plus a box of groceries, a shaving kit, a pair of socks, and a half dozen wineglasses. He made the best break, the best seam, and the straightest furrow. Now he patterns his field in long, perfectly matching lines. Behind him, settling in white rows on the freshly turned, dark-brown earth, seagulls gather at a banquet of grubs and worms – a sight that is not extraordinary even in the heart of the mainland, for the sea penetrates Scotland so deeply on all sides that farmers and crofters in far-inland glens can scarcely break the soil before the furrows behind them turn white with gulls.

The mail comes toward noon. The deliverer is Angus MacFadyen, who is referred to by everyone on the island as Angus the Post. He drives a bright-red Land-Rover that has the words 'Royal Mail' exquisitely lettered on its sides in Post Office gold. Angus the Post has long dark hair, neatly combed. He is a handsome man, with a classical nose and a smile that can dry rain before it hits the ground. He is a singer with a beautiful voice, and once won a singing prize in the regional Mod. There is a touch of show business about him. 'Bye, bye just now,' he says, and away goes the Royal Mail. He stops at the gate of the croft, gets out, opens the gate, gets back into the Land-Rover, drives through the gate, gets out, closes the gate, gets back in, and drives on. Angus the Post has star quality. The General Post Office pays him eight pounds a week, for three days' delivering. The island postmaster, who works all week long, gets six pounds fourteen shillings.

While the gate was open and Angus was driving through it, a bicycle passed him, going in the other direction. The itinerant peddler has come to the croft. He visits the island several times a year, and spends four days riding his rounds. As saddlebags, he carries a thickly packed leatherboard suitcase and a bundle of goods rolled in a small tarpaulin. His bicycle looks like a thin mule. He has a plaid cap, an old tweed jacket. He wears high-topped shoes, and to protect his legs from the bicycle chain he has wrapped them in the way that soldiers wrapped their legs during the First World War. He is old enough to remember that, and perhaps to have done it. Margaret greets him with the news that he is going to sell her nothing, but she allows him to unstrap his suitcase and his canvas bundle, and to unpack them in her kitchen. She sits in a chair; he kneels on the floor – John Karem, peddler, versus Margaret MacMillan Mac-Arthur McNeill. He shows her a cardigan. 'It's lovely,' she says. 'What else have you got?' He shows her lumber-jackets, shirts, lacy nylon nightgowns, and Shetland-wool pullovers for fifty shillings apiece. 'They're lovely,' she says. 'What else have you got?'

These itinerant peddlers used to go from house to house telling stories – part Homer, part drummer. They told tales of mermaids, fairies, seal women, and the warriors of the clans. When millers, weavers, tailors, and shoemakers lived on the island, earlier in this century, they used to go around from house to house telling stories, too. One of these was Big Tailor, a well-remembered man. Big Tailor was more than a raconteur. He was a story in himself. He lived alone near Port Mor (Big Harbour), within sight of the McNeills' croft. He went everywhere on crutches, and he explained that he was so big that he needed them to help hold himself up. He was, indeed, gross in almost all dimensions as he appeared before the other people of the island, measuring them for the clothes he would sew. He had the thighs, hips, waist, and shoulders of an inflated effigy at a fair. Then, late one night, he was seen in the moonlight. He left his house, without the crutches, and walked to a well for water. He was a skinny little man, was Big Tailor.

The itinerant peddler fails completely with Margaret. In a burst of sympathetic generosity, I buy a handkerchief from him for one shilling and sixpence. He opens the drawstring of a pale-blue woollen moneybag, puts the two coins inside, and draws the string shut.

The doctor has had an unfortunate accident while on his way to get his milk at the home farm, Kiloran, the laird's farm. Free milk from the laird's cows is one of the perquisites the doctor enjoys in return for being here at all, and it is the sum of the deference that is shown to him. He says that when he came here, years ago, he was accustomed to the atmosphere of deferential respect that a doctor ordinarily moves about in on the mainland, and that he found none of it on Colonsay. The doctor, tall and spare, is a thinker, and his mind drifts. As he neared the laird's farm in his Land-Rover, his thoughts were far, far away. After a long straight stretch, the road takes a hairpin turn to the left, and there the doctor made a slight right. Crashing through a hedge and across a garden, he opened a huge longitudinal crack in the front wall of the house of Roger McIntyre, who works for the laird. A similar crack opened in the doctor's head. No one was home at the McIntyres'. The doctor remembers nothing of what happened during the next half hour, but he left a great deal of blood in Roger McIntyre's garden, and pools of it were later found in the Land-Rover. Bleeding so profusely, amnesic and distraught, the doctor nonetheless backed his Land-Rover through the hedge, and, as if nothing had happened, went on to collect his milk. No one saw him. The milk itself told the story, the milk bottles and several empty prescription bottles (people who live on or near Kiloran farm take advantage of the doctor's daily routine to have their prescriptions refilled), for he picked up the milk and the empty bottles, spilling blood all over the dairy, and routinely drove home, where his wife looked after him.

The doctor says that this story is extraordinary only in that no one saw him. It is now a week since the accident, and he said this morning, from under a cap of gauze, 'This is the only event I know of, since I've been here, that no one witnessed. They're an extremely observant people here. You can't go out without someone noticing it and recording it in their minds.'

Colonsay is less like a small town than like a large lifeboat. By a scale of things that begins with cities and runs to hamlets, the island is some distance off the end. The usual frictions, gossip, and intense social espionage that characterize life in a small town are so grandly magnified on Colonsay that they sometimes appear in surprising form, in the way that patches of skin

magnified a hundred diameters may appear to be land-
scapes of the moon. Air and water, sea and sky, life is
imploded upon the people here by the blue bottle that
surrounds them. Everyone is many things to everyone
else, and is encountered daily in a dozen guises. En-
meshed together, the people of the island become one
another. Friend and enemy dwell in the same skin. It
has been said to me, for example – but never by either of
the two men – that Donald Gibbie and Angus the Post
share a deep and ramifying antipathy, and that this
showed itself most notably when the new pier was built
and Angus the Post became an applicant for pier
master, a job for which Donald Gibbie had apprenticed
himself through years of loading people, sheep, and
cattle into the ferries that met the steamer. Where I
come from, a few angry words at a party can separate
people for all time, but no amount of enmity could do
that on Colonsay, where the sea is close in four directions and where vehicles meet and pass on a road that is
eight feet wide. When the Lochiel approaches over the
water, Donald the pier master is waiting on the pier, and
so is Angus the Post. They have to see each other almost
every day. Each life eclipses the other. They compete in
the rental of space to visitors. They are, among other
things, cousins. A smile always comes to the croft with
the mail. 'Good morning. A nice morning. A nice day.'
Enmity may come with it, but it can be only one of many
threads, and the same threads seem to run from each
person on the island to half the others. The people are
rubbed together beyond the meaning of friction. Deep
feelings are not always relevant. The surface dominates,
because it is so small. Eruptions are spectacular and
brief. 'That's what it's like on this island,' the doctor told
me. 'A great row. A great to-do. A most awful battle.
Then, a day later, it's over.' And the mail keeps coming.

Colonsay's physical perspectives are in some ways

similar to its human ones. Things amplify. It may be the light. The cairns at the summits of the hills appear from below to be as large as fortresses, at the very least, but if you go up there and stand on them they are only piles of stones, roughly six feet cubed. Shepherds built the cairns for guidance in the mists. The best way to know the island whole is to climb to the cairns in clear weather. Seventeen square miles in eight minutes of latitude may be the next thing to nothing, but after a short time it becomes a continent. The hills, nearly all of them treeless, have the scale and appearance of mountain ranges, walling off one area from another in the way that mountains will divide two states or countries. And that is what the parts of Colonsay suggest – separate states, separate territories. The northernmost of these areas is cut off from the rest of the island by a range that runs from coast to coast, and, from the summit of the highest hill, Carn an Eoin (the Bird Cairn), one looks far down into a remote green valley dotted with sheep and surrounded on its three other sides by high rock formations that shelter the valley from the sea. The name of this place is Balnahard. The 'd' is silent. One family lives there, on 1,268 acres. The distance from Balnahard to the Ardskenish Peninsula is only about six miles, but it feels ten times that and, from Carn an Eoin, can appear to be. People on Colonsay sometimes visit one another for several days, in the expressed belief that they live too far apart for visits of shorter duration. When the doctor crashed into the house of Roger McIntyre, Roger McIntyre and his family had gone to Balnahard for the weekend.

Balnahard and Balavetchy, Uragaig, Kiloran, Kilchattan, Bonaveh, Scalasaig, Machrins, Balaromin Dhu, Balaromin Mor, Garvard, Ardskenish, and Oronsay are the whole of the island, north to south, and are also its thirteen original colonies. Oronsay, half the time, is an island itself, cut off at high tide by seven feet of water over a wide strip of sand. Most of the people and most of the island's structures are in Scalasaig (the doctor, the minister, Angus the Post, the inn, the store, the pier, the Church of Scotland) and in the crofting townships, Uragaig and Kilchattan (the 'c' is silent), where Donald Gibbie lives. From freshwater lakes, streams trail out to the sea. At least three of the lakes are thick with trout. A fourth one has bass. It is a high tarn in a cup of the hills, called Loch a' Sgoltaire (Loch of the Cleaver), and in the centre of it is a small island. The clansmen of Colonsay long ago built a fort on this island as a refuge from attacking MacLeans. Just beneath the water's surface a causeway led out to the fort, but along such a zigzagging route that only an experienced foot could follow it. MacLeans fell off, sank in their chain-mail shirts, and drowned. Donald Gibbie told me that during the Second World War the old laird and his wife, Lord and Lady Strathcona, put all their family silver and jewels into a small boat one moonlit night and rowed out to the island in Loch a' Sgoltaire, where they buried their treasure against the possibility of the coming of a new invader. 'Some say it is still there,' Donald said, 'but the Strathconas aren't made that way, I can tell you.'

Almost every rise of ground, every beach, field, cliff, gully, cave, and skerry has a name. There are a hundred and thirty-eight people on Colonsay, and nearly sixteen hundred place names. In the time of the chiefs and before the age of formal crofting, men used to climb hills in the spring and decide who, this year, would use what pieces of ground, and where, at the water's edge, they would fish. Their eye for minor landmarks became acute – Murrach Mor (the Big Bent-Covered Hillock), Aodann Mor Thurnigil (the Big Rock Face at Twisting Gully), Teanga na Dubhaird (the Tongue of the Black Cape). All these names are preserved in the memories of the people (and also in a book compiled by the laird's uncle and on a map of the island six feet high, eight hundred and eighty feet to the inch, property of the laird). The names commemorate events, revive special interests and proprietary claims of lives long gone, and sketch the land in language: Caolas nan Locharnach (the Norsemen's Channel), Bogha nan Diurach (the Reef of the Jura Men), Bealach Pholl a' Ghlearain (the Pass of the Yellow-Rattle Pool), Gleann Raon a' Bhuilg (the Glen of the Baglike Plain), Sgeir na Tuathail (the Skerry of the North-Facing Creek), Sguid nam Ban Truagh (the Shelter of the Miserable Women), Teampull a' Ghlinne (the Temple of the Glen), Carraig Chaluim Bhain (Fair Malcolm's Fishing Rock), Carraig Ghill-easbuig Ruaidh (Red Archibald's Fishing Rock), Carraig Nighean Mhaol Choinnich (Bald Kenneth's Daughter's Fishing Rock), Carraig Sail nam Partan (the Fishing Rock of the Crabfish's Heel), Tobar a' Gharaidh Bhric (the Well of the Speckled Thicket), Tobar a' Bhainne Dheirg (the Well of the Red Trickle), Lodan Lobh (Foul Puddle), Port Lobh (Foul Harbour), Aoineadh Beag Ceann a' Gharaidh (the Little Terrace at the Head of the Dike), A' Chlach Thogalaich (the Lifting Stone), a boulder once used to prove the strength of young islanders, who were considered men when they could lift it (the custom ended fairly recently, when the better part of a generation developed hernias), A' Chloich Thuill (the Pierced Stone), which cured consumption if the sufferer walked around the stone three times reciting verses, then lay down in the incoming tide, Creag na Teasaiche (Fever Rock), Carragh Mhic a' Phi (McPhee's Standing Stone), Slochd Dubh Mhic a' Phi (McPhee's Black Gully), six different places called Leab' Fhalaich Mhic a' Phi (McPhee's Hiding Bed), Bun a' Bheithe (the Foot of the Birch Wood), Earr an Rudha Bhric (Extremity of the Speckled Point), Pairc Aonghais Ruaidh (Red Angus's Field), Lon Bata Shomhairle Leith

(Grey Samuel's Boat Pool), Saobhshruth Eilean nan Corp (the Corpse Island Eddy), Eilean Ban Scalasaig (the Island of the Scalasaig Women), Clais nam Faochag (the Periwinkle Cleft), An t-Easan Dubh (the Little Black Waterfall), Poll Eadar da Pholl (the Pool Between Two Pools), Lochan a' Laoigh Bhain (the Little Loch of the White Calf), Laosnaig Tonbhan (the White-Rumped Extremity), Uamh na Bantighearna (the Lady Cave), An Uamh Ghabhach (the Danger Cave), Tobhtachan Aonghais an Dobhaidh (the Ruins of the House of Boisterous Angus), Tobhta Dhonnchaidh an Oir (the Ruins of the House of Duncan of the Gold).

In Uragaig — seagirt Uragaig, cut off by mountains, like Balnahard — there is a jutting cliff that rises a hundred feet above the water, and the top of it is relatively flat and covered with grass. A fort stood there once — traceries of similar fortifications are on most of the principal headlands around the island — and the ramparts are now just heavy welts under the grass, kept visible by the nibbling of sheep. Beyond the ramparts, a pinnacle of rock reaches out from the escarpment like a bowsprit. On Sunday, in the course of a long and circuitous walk, Donald Gibbie stepped out onto this rock spar, turned around, and stood there for a minute or two on one foot. His wife begged him to get off, but he ignored her. He might have been a Mohawk on a high girder, and he seemed even less concerned than a Mohawk would be by the peril of his position. Grinning at his wife's worry, wind blowing in his face, he said that in an era when the island had been under the ownership of McNeill lairds, prior to the establishment of the present lairdship, this pinnacle of rock had served a ceremonial purpose. The McNeill lairds used to go out there every so often and stand over the sea on one foot, for long periods of time, to prove to man and nature that they were superior human beings.

Margaret said that she had heard the story often and believed no part of it.

Coming in off the arm of rock, Donald said, 'If I tell a lie, a lie has been told unto me.'

Margaret's face seemed to reflect a mixture of relief at Donald's return to safety and ridicule towards his story of the lairds. 'It's wonderful, right enough,' she said.

The McNeill lairds were McNeills of Gigha, another Hebridean island, and when they came, with their clansmen, they added their name to that of all the descendants of John of the Ocean, with the result that in modern times there is a high proportion of McNeills (in variant spellings) in the population of Colonsay. There are now so many McNeills, in fact, that the name has become all but useless as a means of identification. In many instances it has been replaced in a manner that recapitulates some of the earliest beginnings of sur-names. Donald MacNeill of Garvard, for example, is known throughout the island as Donald Garvard, and never as anything else. His wife, Joan, is Joan Garvard. Andrew Macneill of Oronsay is universally known as Andrew Oronsay. He happened to marry a MacNeill, Donald Garvard's sister Flora MacNeill, and she is now known as Flora Oronsay. Roger McNeill of Machrins is called Roger Machrins. His daughter Mary is Mary Mach-rins. Roger Machrins, an uncle of Donald Garvard and Flora Oronsay, is a first cousin once removed of Donald McNeill of Kilchattan, who is known as Donald Gibbie (son of Gilbert). He could not be known as Donald Kilchattan because Kilchattan is a crofting township and there are a number of families and crofts there, while Oronsay, Machrins, and Garvard are worked only by single farming families. Donald Gibbie's grandmother was a sister of Donald Garvard's grandfather Neil Ban McNeill, among whose sons was not only Roger Mach-rins but also Angus Balaromin Mor. All this is only a fragment of Donald Gibbie's chart of relatives. On the cliff in Uragaig, he said, 'I think you may say that I am related to practically everybody on the island.'

There are a number of McAllisters, too, and one Peter McAllister is known as Peter Bella, since he is married to a woman named Bella. She, in turn, is known as Bella Peter. Another Peter McAllister, a heavy young man, is known as Big Peter, or, alternatively, as Peter Mary Ann. Another Mary McAllister, a cousin of Peter Mary Ann, is called Mary Calum Coll – for her father, Calum, and her grandfather, Coll. Balnahard, incidentally, is farmed by an incomer, a Lowland Scot named Peter Kelly, who is known throughout the island as Peter Kelly. 'With a name like that, he needs no nickname,' says Donald Gibbie.

Just as Colonsay is a small continent, some of its men cut rather disproportionately prominent figures against the sky. Under the brooding absence of the laird, there are great men here, within their context – masters, for a few pounds' rent a year, of considerable domains, with an independence that must go beyond any usual sense of that word elsewhere, except on another remote small island. I have heard them say, with no note of daring or flippancy in their voices or of any doubt whatever, that there is nothing an incomer could teach an islander. In this world, it is true.

———————————

Donald Garvard – who is a big and powerful man, with speckled skin and a handsome, weathered face – strides alongside his two dozen beef cattle in a heavy mist on the grasslands of Balaromin Mor, reddish-grey-brown curly hair streaming out behind his knitted cap, a crook in his hand. He looks like an actor, and he talks like one, with a baritone greeting. He removes his cap. There is no hair beneath it. He has the most luxuriant fringe in Scotland.

Resident in Garvard, he has long since annexed the grazings of Balaromin Mor, and he also works a croft in Kilchattan for an elderly aunt and uncle – in all, some fifteen hundred acres. Donald Garvard is probably the only farmer or crofter in the history of Colonsay who has gone to a public school. At Keil, in Dunbartonshire, he played second-row forward on the Rugby football club, and was a cruncher in the scrum against lads from places like Dollar and Glasgow Academies. In a sense, Keil was not his first boarding school, for he was born on Oronsay, the son of Calum Oronsay, and because of the problem of the isolating tides he took a horse on Sunday afternoons and went to Scalasaig, where he boarded with a family during the week so that he could go to the Colonsay school.

Around the age of fifteen, when he was at Keil, he developed a desire to become an actor. 'I really had not an ambition but a yen to act,' he has told me, and, regardless of what that distinction may have meant, he planned to go to London and to try to make his name in the West End. The Second World War came, and he went instead to western Canada, where he was trained as a Royal Air Force bomber pilot; and during one leave he made a pilgrimage to Hollywood, by car, hugging a cake of ice as he crossed the Nevada desert. The war years changed him, and when the war was over he weighed the London stage on the one hand and the life of Colonsay on the other, and he chose to go home. He took with him a young wife, a redhead like himself. He called her Joanie Pony. Born Joan Turnbull ('a turbulent border family'), she had been working in the choruses of shows in Glasgow when they met.

'Pony and I came back and we set up a wee wooden house in Kilchattan,' he said one day.

'We lived in a stable for two years,' said Joan.

'Then Garvard became vacant,' he went on. 'The

laird asked me if I would like to come here.'

They raised two children (both now in secondary school on the mainland), and Joan Garvard learned Gaelic so well, and sang it so beautifully, that she nearly won a gold medal in the National Mod. She is an ample woman with an affectionate sense of humour and a gusty laugh. Donald Garvard meanwhile began to write poetry in Gaelic, and still does. But he feels hemmed in by it. 'If you try to describe a day like this, what you see out on the hill, you have, in Gaelic, few adjectives,' he complained. 'I would like to have more. Anyway, I'm very happy with my Pony now, whipping around. Some days I'm at the absolute zenith of enjoyment, and the next day I'm at the absolute nadir of despondency.'

Joan said, 'That all depends whether you are manic or depressive.'

They have twenty-five breeding cows and four hundred breeding ewes. They make money. 'All the farms make money except Kiloran, the home farm,' Donald Garvard said. 'Oh, aye, we have an economic problem on this island. The new laird doesn't want to spend money here the way his father did. But you can judge him for yourself. He'll be here soon enough. The islanders' current fear is that they don't know what is going to happen to the island. The population has been cut in half in the past ten years. What we may need is a distillery. It would cost two hundred and fifty thousand pounds and it would employ no more than ten men, but it would occasion more steamers coming to the island, and that would lower freight costs and fuel costs. I have a feeling that things will be all right. I would like to think that I could stay here until I die.'

In a context of individualism, Donald Garvard is particularly individualistic, like his father, Colum Oronsay, who used to stir mayonnaise into his coffee. Donald Garvard sometimes wears shorts, polo shirts, and red slippers. If his feet are cold when he is visiting at someone's house, he will lie down on the floor and stick his legs into the oven. People around the island seem to talk about him more than they do about almost anyone else with the possible exception of the laird and Andrew Oronsay.

'Donald Garvard is a generous man. He would lend his last hundred pounds.'

'He comes in like a bit of a breeze.'

'He's a hail fellow.'

'He has a strong, Highland sense of humour.'

'He's a deep thinker, a seeker after truth and knowledge.'

'Aye, he has used his education to good purpose intellectually.'

'I've had some quite deep philosophic talks with him – I mean, right down to it.'

'On the other hand, Donald Garvard can be a bastard, and when Donald Garvard's got a bucket in him, he can be a pest of hell.'

'Aye, he likes a tot of whisky.'

'When he is halfway over, he is great company.'

'He is the most friendly person on the island, but occasionally when he is in his cups he takes off his jacket to have a go with his fists.'

'I think, between ourselves, that Donald Garvard married money. In fact, he did marry money, and when he's in his cups he makes no bones about it.'

'That sounds a bit near the bone.'

'Joan has a touch of the snob about her – and so does Donald Garvard.'

'Joan out-islands many of the islanders.'

'She is a better grammarian than Donald Garvard in Gaelic.'

'They spend a great deal of money on tobacco and whisky.'

'Aye.'

'He is a constant actor, and should be on the stage.'

'Donald Garvard used to go around in an old Glasgow taxi he had that was tied together with string and wire. One night after a gun-club shoot, when it was dark and he'd had a dram or two, he borrowed torches to use as headlamps, and he started for Garvard. The taxi went into a ditch, and the torches went out, by the hill at Milbuie. Donald ran up the hill. He says that he sometimes runs to stay upright. He kept on, and he was going over another hill, in Garvard, when he tripped in the heather, fell, and went to sleep. He awoke some time later and went on to his house. "Is that you, Donald?" Joan called out. And he said, "Aye." And she said, "Go milk the cow." Donald sprayed milk from the udder in all directions and whitewashed the inside of the byre.'

'Donald Garvard is a bit irresponsible and will never make a good farmer.'

I sat one noon on a cliff near the top of Ben Oronsay, which rises prominently from the edge of The Strand, the amphibious acreage that separates Oronsay from Garvard and Balaromin Mor. In cold rain and cold sunshine, I ate a piece of lamb, some Islay Mini-Dunlop cheese, shortbread, and white chocolate, and looked to the south across a thousand acres of grazing land, flat and green and as isolated as Balnahard. The grazing, covered with sheep and cattle, was framed by converging rocky shorelines that met in a distant point, the end of the island. Beyond the tip, a small following drop, was Eilean nan Ron (Seal Island). Grey seals by the hundred are born there in late summer. It was among the skerries around this islet that the last Colonsay chief was found in hiding – his presence announced by seagulls screaming above his head – on the day that he was taken across

The Strand to Balaromin Mor and killed. Just below the cliffs of Ben Oronsay, in shelter from northerly winds, a priory was built in the Middle Ages, and its chapels, halls, and cloisters are only partly gone. Stones were taken from the priory in more recent times for use in the construction, on adjacent ground, of Oronsay farmhouse and its steadings. As I looked down from the cliff, I saw, among the ruins of some of the most interesting ecclesiastical structures in the Hebrides, a man and two sheepdogs – the dogs black and lupine, part wolf, or so they seemed, and part collie. The man had a crook in his hand, a visored tweed cap on his head: Andrew Oronsay. I had not met him, but as he moved around below me, I remembered the things I had heard about him.

When people talk about Andrew Oronsay, the stories usually reflect their considerable regard for the diversity of his skills and talents, and the finesse with which he applies them. Affectionately remembered is the day when Andrew almost drowned the factor – Findlay the Factor, who is no longer on the island. It is recalled, as well, that Andrew was an expert in unarmed combat during the Second World War. He is said to be an excellent Highland dancer. And during the bygone era of the annual sheepdog trials – the dogs had to go through three sets of gates, around their owners, and into pens – Andrew Oronsay's dogs traversed the course so fast and so faultlessly that they always won and eventually made the competition irrelevant. As a speaker of two tongues, Andrew Oronsay is credited with eloquence in both, and in Gaelic or English he is said to be as facile with coarse words as with smooth ones. The summer guests at the inn in Scalasaig tend to be energetic women in their fifties and sixties, mainly from Glasgow and Edinburgh, with powdery hair and walking sticks; and almost all of them sooner or later visit Oronsay Priory. When these women tire of looking at Celtic crosses and beautiful tombstones with hinds and hounds and swords and galleys and twining ivy in relief, they look at Andrew Oronsay. They lean on stone fences or stand in the doorway of his threshing shed and sometimes attempt to communicate with him as he performs the business of his farm. Some of Andrew's friends say that although he is ordinarily a polite and gracious man he does not like people watching him as he works, and when people do watch him he swears lightly at first, letting the words patter around just under his breath, and then, after a time, he gets the words up there on his breath at a high mutter, and, with a little more time, a little more watching, the language rises and eventually breaks into a thoroughgoing crescendo that drives all the women back up the road, stilting along like scared blue herons.

One other talent is frequently mentioned. In any place as small and remote as Colonsay, it is unusual in modern times to find someone who can play the great Highland bagpipes even competently, let alone well, and it is thus almost unbelievable that there lives on the island – in a population of a hundred and thirty-eight – a piper of the magnitude of Andrew Oronsay. He once lived on the mainland, and although he is too modest to admit it he is said to have played at the launching of the R.M.S. Queen Elizabeth, at Clydebank, and to have been singled out for congratulations by the Queen Mother. Pipers have genealogies, lines of pedagogical ancestry, that are as important to them as bloodlines may be to others. A piper schooled in classical *piobaireachd* – or *ceol mor*, the purest expression of Highland bagpipe music – can listen to another piper and say accurately who his teachers were and who, in turn, taught the teachers. A Scottish bagpiper might be traced to, say, the Macintyres of Atholl or to the Rankins of Duart and Coll, but he can have among his aesthetic forebears no greater men than the Mac-Crimmons of Skye, hereditary pipers to the MacLeods of

MacLeod. Donald Mor MacCrimmon, born in 1570, taught his son, Patrick Mor MacCrimmon, who taught *his* son, Patrick Og MacCrimmon, who felt that his father and grandfather were guilty of ever-increasing excessive embellishment and therefore purified what he had learned by stripping it down to classical standards that have stood for nearly three hundred years. Pipers, in the era of the clans, were so important that they were given servants to carry the pipes. Patrick Og MacCrimmon taught John Dall Mackay of Gairloch, a blind piper (*'dall'* means 'blind') who died in 1754, eight years after Culloden and as many years after the playing of the great Highland bagpipes had been declared an act of treason. John Dall Mackay had already taught his son, Angus, and this Angus Mackay, treason immaterial, later taught John Mackay of Raasay, who was born in 1767, twenty-one years after Culloden. John Mackay of Raasay, who was a clansman but not any sort of immediate relative of his teacher, passed along his craft and art to his son, Angus Mackay. By now, piping was in open and ceremonial revival, with much made of it by the Highland Society of London, in memory of the clans. Felix Mendelssohn was imitating the sound of the pipes in his 'Scotch Symphony'. And Angus Mackay eventually became piper to Queen Victoria. He also went insane, and finally drowned himself in an asylum. ('There are,' someone once said to me, 'a lot of wee stories about them all.') One of the first to record the *ceol mor* in staff notation, Angus Mackay had also been the teacher of Donald Cameron. Donald Cameron taught Alexander Cameron, who taught John MacDougall Gillies, who taught Robert Reid, who taught Andrew Oronsay.

I made my way down from the cliff to meet him. He was a short man with a round, weather-reddened face. He looked youthful, although his hair was grey. He had a moustache. His eyes were blue and quick and bright, but they turned aside at times in shyness. When I introduced myself to him, he spoke in an extraordinarily soft voice and said that he was glad that I had come for a wee visit, for he had heard of me from his brother-in-law, Donald Garvard, and also from Donald Gibbie. 'You're wet and cold,' he said. 'You must come in and dry off and have a cup of tea.'

The legs of my trousers were soaked from the high heather and the patches of mushy ground that I had gone through on my way up Ben Oronsay. The water had gone down inside my boots. I was shivering, so I followed him without trying to disclaim what he said. I told him that I thought his sheepdogs, which circled us as we walked, were fine-looking animals.

'They're intelligent, anyway,' he said. 'You can speak to them and tell them there are three sheep in a certain place, and they will go and get them. But the price of their intelligence is that every so often they go mad and kill sheep. Not terribly long ago, two of them – not these two – killed forty in one night.'

The path he followed curved along the low stone fence of the graveyard by the priory church, whose walls were still standing, with tufts of grass growing high above the ground from chinks in the rotting stone. The church was roofless, like most of the other buildings, but the mullions in its principal window were still intact, and they divided three lanciform lights, tall and slim. In the graveyard were two Celtic crosses. Andrew said that one cross dated only to the sixteenth century but that the other had been carved in the ninth century. Bits of headstones and tombstones were scattered all over the graveyard, having become disengaged long since from the turf that covered the bones they once commemorated. 'This place is full of your people,' Andrew said. 'Would you like to see the best stones? They were taken away and put under shelter.' He crossed to the far side of the priory and went into a building that had once been the barn and byre, and had been given a new roof some forty years ago so that the slabs of the dead could be preserved there. The tombstones were spaced out on the floor in long rows, each stone about six feet long and covered with carving in relief. Andrew showed me the one that he thought was the most beautiful. It was the tombstone of the chief who was killed by the MacLean arrow in the cave – or 'black gully' – that still bears his name. The stone showed a stag surrounded by dogs, and a griffin, and below that a sword garlanded with foliage, and below that a galley in full sail. Andrew said that the ship and the sword had traditionally represented the Lords of the Isles, and *only* the Lords of the Isles – something that no man of Colonsay had ever come near to being. 'But at the time of this one's death,' he said, 'there was some dubiety as to who actually was the Lord of the Isles, so he nipped in smartly and put the galley and the sword on his tombstone.'

I told Andrew that even in recent times there had been people in my family who would do things like that.

'Are there many Highland people in your area?' he said.

I thought of some people I had known – Roger MacLean, Audrey MacPherson, Laura MacMillan, Russ McNeill, David McAlpin, Robbie Campbell, Jim Cameron, Corning Chisholm, Ruth Mackay, Godfrey MacDonald – and I said, 'Some, I guess. To tell you the truth, I have never really thought of them that way.'

Five pictures hung on the walls of Andrew's sitting room. Two, in handsome frames, were of sheep. A third, even more handsomely mounted, was a portrait of a sheepdog. The two others were striking photographic reproductions of rubbings from Oronsay tombstones, including the one of the chief who had tried to nip in on the Lordship of the Isles. Andrew gave me woollen socks and a pair of trousers, and when I had changed from my own socks and trousers his wife spread them over a chair by a coal fire to dry. Flora Oronsay, a solid and attractive woman, had the auburn hair of her brother, Donald Garvard, and the same easy-going, affable manner. Flora and Andrew were married in 1947, I would eventually learn, and the wedding party crossed at low tide to Oronsay for the reception and stayed for twelve hours, wandering back across The Strand at the next low tide, weaving and swaying in the heavy mists in the small hours of the morning. For five years, Flora and Andrew had run The Shop, in Scalasaig, and had then taken over at Oronsay, where now, the sole inhabitants are the two of them and her mother, Ina Oronsay, a strong and constantly grinning woman of ninety. They live on some fourteen hundred acres, cut off by hill and tide, and when I first visited them the two women had not crossed The Strand, had not gone even to Garvard, let alone to Scalasaig, for the better part of a year.

Flora and Ina Oronsay set dinner on the kitchen table. The tea Andrew had mentioned was supplemented by eggs, sausages, pancakes, scones, and round slices of bread that had been baked in a tubular tin, which had once held the dried milk that is shipped from the mainland to the school. The women of Colonsay are bakers of great skill, and they have to be, because they are so far from the nearest baker's shop. In any Colonsay house, at least six meals are served each day, and into the people and their visitors go an incredible number of drop scones, blueberry scones, oven scones, girdle scones, potato scones, pancakes, spongecakes, creamcakes, oatcakes, chocolate cakes, mince pies, Madeira cakes, rock cakes, and clootie-dumpling fruitcakes. That particular day, I tried to excuse myself by saying that I had only recently eaten my lunch, but that made no impression, and I was soon inflated with scones.

While we ate, I asked Andrew if he found island farming profitable enough, and he told me that it was all right but nothing more, that he had six hundred and thirty sheep, thirty cows, and a bull, and that his sales of calves and lambs had brought him thirteen hundred pounds the previous year. 'It is easy to be romantic about the Highlands,' he said. 'People from the mainland come here in the summer and say what a free and open country life it is, but when they come here for a winter and get a little mud up their backs, the romantic part of it is all over. It's difficult to keep people interested in the islands.'

I remarked that his pastures looked beautiful just now.

'It's rough-grazing,' he said. 'The word "pasture" to me conveys something more succulent than what we have here.'

Towards the end of the meal his wife asked me, 'Do many Highland people live where you do?'

I told her what I had earlier told Andrew.

Andrew said, 'Do many pipers live near you?'

And I said, 'No. We hear them in parades once in a while, and in Scottish shows in Madison Square Garden.'

'The Black Watch played the pipes in President Kennedy's funeral,' he said. 'I have heard a record of it, and they did not play well.'

After a moment, I said, 'As a matter of fact, I haven't heard any pipers on Colonsay.'

'I used to play,' he said. 'But I don't play much anymore.'

'I've been told that you are quite good,' I said.

'Och, they tell stories,' Andrew said. 'I haven't played in months – years.'

Flora and Ina Oronsay laughed. I said I hoped to hear a piper sometime.

'Would you like a wee tune?' he said, looking past me and into the floor.

From another room he brought his pipes, and he assembled them in the kitchen, the metal surfaces of each one being as clear as mirrors. They fitted together with lathed threads, like the tubes of some precision instrument, which, in a sense, they were. Andrew then filled the bag with air and stepped into the stone-surfaced courtyard outside his kitchen door. The sun was shining again. The first sound was a giant monotone – the basic air release – and it was a sound that seemed big enough to scatter clouds. Then melody rode over the top, high lingering notes coming so slowly that they seemed to be growing from the pipes. Andrew, with a look of pained concentration, turned slowly as he played, clockwise, his face in sun and then in shadow. He was playing 'Over the Sea to Skye', and when he finished that he played 'The Road to the Isles'. A scruffy black-and-white cat crouched beside him. His shepherd's crook leaned against the garden wall behind him.

When he had finished, we went back to the sitting room, where he disassembled the pipes and, while he did so, told me that the bagpipe as an instrument had not changed since the seventeenth century, that the high era of bagpipe composition had passed before 1800, and that the Courts of Justice had once ruled that a man carrying bagpipes was a man carrying a weapon – so inspiring was the music of the pipers to the clans in battle. He said that *ceol mor* consists of traditionally structured themes and groundwork, to which individuals attach their own variations, and that young pipers often exasperate him because they leave out fundamental elements. He showed me his basic text of *piobaireachd*, *The Kilberry Book of Ceol Mor*. As I turned the pages slowly, he hummed some of the tunes that went by, and the tunes he was humming were so sad, beautiful, lilting, and melodic that I found myself wondering if, when these themes emerged from the great Highland bagpipes, Andrew could hear something that I could not. My ear is not a good one for the sound of the pipes. The possibility crossed my mind that there might be some congenital difference in the architecture of our ears. Perhaps he had a double, a triple, a braided auditory nerve that evolution had prepared for the piper alone. My ear, on the other hand, was more than receptive to the sound of the names of the great *ceol-mor* tunes that were now passing before me on the pages of the book, and I remember thinking that if I was deprived of some of the magic of the sound of the pipes I could hear at least the roll of the titles – 'The Lament for Red Hector of the Battles', 'MacDonald of Kinlochmoidart's Lament', 'Salute on the Birth of Rory Mor MacLeod', 'The Glen Is Mine', 'In Praise of Morag', 'Clanranald's Salute', 'Lady Margaret MacDonald's Salute', 'The Battle of the Pass of Crieff', 'The Battle of the Bridge of Perth', 'The Lament for Donald Ban MacCrimmon', 'The Sound of the Waves Against the Castle of Duntroon'.

I had crossed to Oronsay as the tide was going out, and it was now time for me to leave. From his house, Andrew can tell by watching a certain point on the western shoreline how much time a visitor has before it is too late to recross The Strand to Balaromin Mor. He said he would give me a ride partway on his tractor, and asked if I would like to have a look inside the church and the cloisters before I left. The church was floored with turf and a ram was grazing there. Andrew said that it was generally thought that St Columba had established the priory in the sixth century, and that most of the present structures had been built on the same site by John, Lord of the Isles, in the fourteenth. Grass grew deep in the cloisters, among three rows of triangular arches and one row of semicircular arches, serene and intact. As we were going out, Andrew bent over and picked up a human occipital bone. 'One of yours, I expect,' he said, and handed it to me. Holding it, I felt nothing more than, perhaps, an affectionate curiosity. Since that day, though, I have found that that moment in the cloister has not left my mind, and that the touch of the grasses, the wet cool of the air, and even the inscriptions on the arches – *'Celestinus Canonicus Huius Operis'* – are more distinct in memory than they seemed to be at the time. I set the occipital piece on a ledge in the cloister wall where there was a small pile of other human bones. 'Tidying up a bit,' Andrew said.

'Yes, tidying up,' I said, and we went to the tractor.

He let me off at a place in the middle of The Strand where a stone cross had once stood, engulfed half the time, but half the time appearing as a sign to anyone who sought sanctuary at the priory. Fugitives from metropolitan Colonsay were beyond pursuit and in utter safety once they passed what became known as the Sanctuary Cross. Only a few broken stones, arranged in the flat sand in the shape of a cross, marked the area now. I said goodbye to Andrew beside these stones, and he turned the tractor around and started back, his tires spraying the perceptibly rising water. The stones of the cross were covered with mussels. I collected as many as I could hold or fit into my pockets and the hood of my rain gear, then ran to beat the tide. We made *moules marinière* that night with malt whisky.

Ross and Neil Darroch have been made redundant. Colonsay is in a state of atrophy, and has been since 1830, when there were a thousand people here, but the atrophy has been accelerated in recent years. The old laird, to preserve the status quo and his peace and quiet, underwrote the Colonsay economy; but the new laird wants the island to pay for itself or, as Andrew puts it, 'he's wanting it to wash his face.' The laird has, among other things, stopped supplying free coal, free undertaking, and free electricity, and he has declared a number of jobs at the home farm redundant, reducing the personnel there by two-thirds – the brothers Ross and Neil Darroch included. The Darrochs are islanders, and they have stayed on Colonsay. But others have left, and before long the population will probably number no more than seventy. There is, at the moment, only one teenage girl on the island, so dances are no longer held. There are only eight people whose ages are between fourteen and twenty-six. Among the older people there is a profound sense of unease about the future of Colonsay, and in their conversations there are frequent allusions to other islands, once inhabited, where the population is now zero – Pabbay, Sandray, Taransay, Scarba, Soay, Mingulay, St Kilda.

'There are about twenty children five and under. There will be no employment for these people, you can see that.'

'Angus the Post has two boys and two girls. The girls are twins. Donald Gibbie has two girls. Angus Balaromin Dhu has a boy and a girl, and his wife is pregnant. Big Peter McAllister has two girls. Alastair Machrins has two boys. In ten years' time, what are they going to do?'

'The sad thing is, if they go, they never come back.'

'Och, yes. The young people leave the island and there is no bringing them back.'

'Donald Garvard has two away. I don't suppose they'll ever come back.'

'Findlay MacFadyen has four sons. They'll all be off this island in two years.'

'There's nothing in Colonsay. You can get work but no pay.'

'Latent but inevitable is the breakdown of the economic fabric of the island.'

'Aye.'

'Two funerals, one wedding – that has been the social life here during the past year.'

One other event brought the whole island out – a conflagration at Kiloran Farm last Boxing Day. It was a spectacular fire, and on the following day a Glasgow newspaper ran a headline that read, 'ISLANDERS STAND BY WHILE LAIRD'S SHED BURNS'. Some say that the headline could be taken at face value, but most say that there was in fact nothing else that the islanders could have done, for the shed was full of dry hay, it burned quickly, the nearest water supply had gone dry, only two hundred feet of hose could be found on the entire island, and of the volunteer firemen of Colonsay – a group that had been organized at least fifteen years earlier – more than half were dead.

When men are made redundant, they find things to do. Ross and Neil Darroch lay bricks. They fix fences. They work in the engine shed at Machrins. They dig ditches for the County Council. They always work together. They always seem to be silhouetted, side by side, not particularly in motion, against the background of the hills. They have spent their lives together. They are tall and lean men, with faces that suggest that not much could alarm them, and they have the slouch of American cowboys. Thirty-five years ago, they crossed the American continent, and recrossed it, as hoboes. Neil Darroch is the strongest man on Colonsay. He can pick up a forty-five-gallon petrol drum and throw it around like a cork.

The petrol drums that he now and then picks up arrive on the Lochiel and are hauled up to the house of the postmaster, Jack Cursiter, who opens them and pours their contents into an underground tank below his Esso pump – the only commercial petrol pump on the island. When a customer comes, Cursiter, who is not a tall or exceptionally strong man, pumps the petrol out of the ground by hand, straining back and forth against a long lever until the customer wonders if Cursiter will collapse before the car's tank is full.

Ross Darroch is an uncompromising companion when he is having a dram at the pub. 'Have a drink,' he says, and if Neil or anyone else says no, Ross says, 'You're *going* to have a drink!' Neil sometimes picks Ross up and tosses him into another part of the room. After a few more rounds in this fashion, Ross sometimes stands to recite 'A bunch of the boys were whooping it up in the Malamute Saloon', and he goes on and on, and Neil listens. The brothers were both married once. Neil's wife died. Ross's wife left him and went to the mainland. Neil and Ross lived in houses side by side when they were married, and they still do. Their friends say that Ross's house now resembles a midden but that Neil's house is neat.

The chief inspector of the Coast Guard for all Great Britain has come to Colonsay to attend a rescue drill, at Machrins. Ten men show up. They are paid a pound apiece for attending drill. They wear rubber rain gear and Wellington boots and look more like fishermen than crofters and farmers. Lining up now, they are, for the most part, not snappy. Moments ago, one of them reached under his slicker, showed me a bottle, and asked if I would like a wee dram. Each wears a white armband with a black number stencilled on it. Donald Gibbie, No. 8, stands straight and attentive as the chief inspector begins to speak. The attention of Ross Darroch, No. 3, wanders at once to some distant point in the Glen of the Baglike Plain, and his gaze becomes fixed, as if he were waiting for something to occur there. The chief inspector, flanked by two officers of the Coast

Guard in Argyll, is a short and lumpy man with grey hair. His dark-blue uniform with its gold loops seems to have been draped around him. He is overweight. Age has found him. He has had to climb to the site of the drill, and now he stops speaking to let his wind restore itself. There is something very likeable about him. He doesn't seem to mind that he stands on lower ground than the men he speaks to. There is noticeable discomfort, however, in the manner of his subordinates, who keep inching toward higher ground after the chief inspector resumes speaking. The two other officers are younger, and they are both good-looking, they have cosmetic dash, and their uniforms are crisp. What dominates the scene, though, is the accent of the chief inspector — awesome, alien, English. His words are covered with gold leaf. They would impress a high table at Cambridge. He is saying that he has been to Colonsay before — fourteen years ago — and he asks who remembers him. Several men speak up, and he warmly shakes their hands. In detail, he begins to describe shipwrecks that have occurred during the past year and that have brought into action local crews like the one before him — off Blyth, in the Orkneys, in the Solway Firth, near Cape Wrath, near the Eddystone Rock, near Flamborough Head. He amplifies the sadness in his tone: '. . . and then she heeled over toward the incoming tide and all were lost.' Ross Darroch wanders off, relieves himself, and returns. The chief inspector tells the group that twenty-three hundred calls to rescue were handled by the Coast Guard last year, and that they should therefore not be nonchalant, for their day is coming. A 'victim' has stretched out on the ground, and one of the younger officers will demonstrate kiss-of-life resuscitation. The young officer says that what one does first is to press on the chest to dislodge anything that happens to be in the throat. 'You've missed out there,' the chief inspector says quickly. He turns to the other officer and asks him to give the correct reason for the pressure on the chest. The other young officer, who has a moustache that somehow suggests a wealth of experience, doesn't know. 'To stimulate the heart. The heart is a massive muscle,' says the chief inspector. 'On with it.' The first young officer bends toward the victim for the kiss of life. His head stops a few inches short. The victim is the man who offered me the dram. 'On with it.' The young officer presses his lips onto the victim's and drives breath into his lungs. 'You've missed out again,' says the chief inspector. 'You forgot to pinch the nose.' Someone fires a rocket that carries with it a nylon line at terrific speed, with the sound of an épée whipping the air. A breeches buoy is set up, and in fast order a 'rescue' is made, a man bobbing in the air between two ledges of rock – 'ship' and 'shore'. The chief inspector is perhaps surprised. He is certainly impressed. He reminds the men that Her Majesty's Government will pay them a pound a head for all souls brought to safety by breeches-buoy rescue. He cites a case where sixty-six persons were saved on the Isle of Lewis. He says, 'Bear in mind, if the Queen Elizabeth ever comes ashore here, you can make twenty-five hundred quid.'

'Well, let's hope she comes ashore, then,' says one of the Colonsay men. 'That will save us all.'

The young minister of the Church of Scotland, according to some islanders, is less interested in salvation than one might expect. It is said that he cares only for those who are already saved. His sermons do not corroborate this. For two weeks now, he has been holding up as an example to this Sunday congregation the conversion and the expanding Christian devotion of the English pop singer Cliff Richard. The congregation is modest.

The small, square, grey church in Scalasaig, with its plain windows, high pulpit, and panelled ceiling, has pew space for about a hundred people. Nineteen were there last time, and six of those were in the choir. Donald Gibbie does not go to church; nor does Margaret. 'We're very irreligious,' Donald says. 'It's a shame we don't attend our church and read our Bible more.' When Donald Gibbie was in England during the Second World War, he was offended that people in Kent shot rabbits on Sunday. But now he thinks of Sunday – and, for that matter, Christmas, too – as just another working day. Charlie McKinnon the Motor Hirer is a regular at the twelve-noon Sunday service. In his small bus, an Austin that seats eleven, he provides free rides for people who want to go to church with him. Colonsay has ten Baptists. Once every three weeks, a Baptist minister visits the island and holds services in the Baptist church, in Kilchattan. Charlie McKinnon charges Baptists full fare. Both Charlie and Angus the Post sing in the Church of Scotland choir. Angus lives two doors away from the church, but he always drives to the services. The young minister is pleased to have been called to the island, for he plans to take advantage of his stay here mainly to cover the great range of reading that will prepare him for his eventual assault on the ecclesiastical bastions of the mainland. In a prayer last Sunday, he reminded God that this is an age of unprecedented communication and asked Him please to make Himself apparent to us. To a slow Caledonian tune, the nineteen of us sang 'The Battle Hymn of the Republic'.

> He has sounded forth the trumpet
> that shall never call retreat;
> He is sifting out the hearts of men
> before His judgment seat . . .

In the sermon that dealt with the pop singer, the minister seemed to be preparing for a last stand – the church back up against the wall, chasing the magic in the world to where it has gone. He also made vague mention of the old laird and the new one, saying, 'Older people may think of the old laird, but younger people think of the new laird, and that is the way things are – generations pass.' The offering was collected in a wooden box. The collector put his own coin in after he had been around to everyone else, and then he held the box under the pulpit, from the height of which the minister's own coins plummeted, making the sound of crashing cymbals when they hit. Last year, the minister performed a wedding, and he took pictures at the reception and sold them to the conjoined families. He is slow to baptize, not being ready to baptize just anyone. He says, 'Baptism is a shell, unless the parents are going to take spiritual command. Then you have the yolk inside.'

Donald Gibbie kills a gull and tacks its white body, smeared with blood, to a fence post on the croft, as a warning to other gulls to stay away from his flocks. When sheep are lambing, there is a moment of danger just after the lambs are born. The ewes are too weak to get up and protect the young. At these times, gulls or crows will sometimes swoop down and peck out the eyes of the lambs. It is spring, and new lambs now cover the island like daisies. Walking in Bonaveh yesterday, my four girls, aged two, four, six, and eight, watched one drop, and petted its warm wet fluff as it hopped around dragging its umbilical cord. The ewe stood close by, but made no attempt to drive them away. When the lambs are a week or two old, they can move like sprinters and shift their field with incredible ease. It is my assignment to catch them, so that Martha, Jenny, Sarah, and Laura can pet them. We do this out on the machair – the natural calcareous grassland that is found on the western side of some of the Hebrides (whence the name Machrins). The machair of Colonsay is so smooth that golf was once played on it. In the game I am now playing, the lambs are superior to me in every important respect, and my only chance is to make them think I am going to the left when I am really going to the right. I stop one in ten. The upshot for the lambs is a pair of warm hands and the touch of children. They seldom fare as well when caught by other creatures. Sarah and I climbed a hill in Balaromin Mor, and on its slopes came upon a ewe standing over a lamb whose abdomen had been ripped open and whose eyes were gone from empty red sockets. The lamb was not a new one; it had been quite well along in weeks. Its body was as warm as in life and its wool was soft and sparkling white. Sarah looked at it for a while, saying nothing. Then she said, 'Is it dead?' I told her I was sure it was, and she said, 'What killed it?' I said, 'I don't know – a gull, I suppose.' And all she said was, 'Oh.' There was no need for explanations. Sarah is six, and she talks about death every day. The ewe had run away from us as we approached and, with amazing speed, had gone up the steep hillside and now stood on a ledge above us, intently watching, black eyes in a black face, looking like a small jousting horse with a white blanket across its back. As we moved away, the ewe returned to the lamb. Donald Gibbie and I made a circuit of the periphery of the Ardskenish Peninsula, collecting mainly eggs and flotsam. We came upon a dead ewe. Donald examined the carcass and said it had been dead for about a week. A lamb was bleating beside it. The lamb's belly was bloated for lack of milk. I suggested that we take it home and try to save it, but Donald said that it was too old to take a bottle, much too old to be transferred to a ewe that had lost its lamb, and probably not old enough to survive on its own. 'With luck, it might make it,' he said, and we moved on. Moments later, we found three plover eggs, two of which we would eat hard-boiled, the other in a batch of pancakes. Donald and I also found five eider-duck eggs – large eggs with beautiful, olive-green shells. He and his wife pickle eider-duck eggs, tern eggs, oyster-catcher eggs, and peewit eggs. Donald carried the five eggs to a pool of water in a basin of rock near the shore. He set them one by one in the water, saying that if they stood on end they were addled. Three stood on end. I poked small holes in them and blew out the interiors, so that I could give the handsome shells to my children. The two others were good to the yolk. Those we would crack and fry.

I have today killed Calum McAllister's chicken, which used to peck around in the environs of the cattle grid where the road crosses the line between Machrins and Kilchattan. Calum McAllister is a cotter – that is, a general hand who is neither crofter nor farmer but makes his living doing jobs where he can find them – and he lives in Machrins, a few yards from the Kilchattan fence line. His chicken made the mistake of jumping up onto the cattle grid a second or two before my car passed over it. News of the death of this chicken apparently reached every ear on the island before the pinfeathers had settled to the ground. It is not a scandal. No one seems to hold it against me. It just is news, and I am already becoming known as the one who killed Calum McAllister's chicken – a description that probably translates into a single word in Gaelic. Looking around, I saw no one coming from Calum McAllister's house, so the first thing I did was to go to the croft to ask Donald Gibbie what the chicken might have been worth. 'I don't know what the legalities are, but we should keep up the goodwill,' Donald Gibbie said. 'I suggest you give Calum twelve bob.' I returned to the cattle grid. The chicken was gone. I knocked on McAllister's door. He opened it – a tall, gaunt, unshaven man, a widower. I said that I had killed his chicken, and he said, 'I know. I know that.'

I said I was very sorry, and he said, 'It's not your fault. It's the chicken's fault. The chicken should not have been in the road.'

'I'd like to give you twelve shillings for the chicken.'

'That is unnecessary.'

'But I think I should pay for it, and I will feel better if you let me do that.'

'You can pay if you like, but the chicken should not have been in the road.'

The air is calm, and the cuckoo sounds from the hills of Balaromin Mor. Below, on The Strand, the tide is low and the hill cows have positioned themselves on the wet flat sand, their forms indistinct in the mist, and they slowly move their heads from side to side. The hill cows are covered with golden hair that is so long it mats their faces entirely and drips down their sides. They are woolly mammoths, gigantic St Bernards, slow-moving hair farms. They are truly unbelievable to any eye that has not seen them before. They are also cattle, inside it all, and there is something mildly electrifying about their presence on The Strand, evidence of intellectual stirrings in those effigial heads, for they could have no other reason for being there than curiosity. The sound of the cuckoo has not stopped. To me it is a novelty – the actual bird's being there in the hills. With every call, it compliments the Swiss, sounding, as it does, exactly like the clock. I have counted, and the last call is No. 66. It is late in the day – 66 p.m. From the cliff where the cuckoo apparently is, an arm of rock reaches out. Centuries ago, a hole was drilled in the outer end of this projection, which has been known since then as the Hangman's Rock. A great many people were hanged there, for offences against the interests of the clan.

Crossing Big Lookout Hill in Scalasaig, I met David

Clark, who had been cutting peat. He was replacing chunks of sod. 'You replace the turf, like a good golfer,' he said. 'Not many people burn peat on Colonsay anymore. Our peat is not of as good quality as the peat of Islay. Everyone burns it there – ministers, doctors. But ours makes a good glow. If you get good weather, it dries just as hard as coal. And what's wrong with a good fire and a book, if it comes to that?' David Clark and his sister Mary Clark share a house beside the church in Scalasaig. They are the retired keepers of the inn there. They are islanders, whose mother's family was of the original clan, and they have shown me the now ruined house in Bonaveh where they were born, with its long vista over the remnants of other houses and then across the water east to the Strait of Corryvreckan, and they seem to regard me as if I had been born in Bonaveh, too, and were only now rising from decades of sleep. Four-year-old Jenny was with me when David was cutting the peat. 'Bye, bye just now,' he said to her as we left. 'I hope you'll manage back soon.'

The sky is royal blue, and below the blue, just above the waves, is a layer of dusty red. Venus is twice as bright and, in this sky, twice as large as Venus is supposed to be. Dusk is collecting, and the stars will show through in a moment. The sun is just gone. In half a minute's time, it will be tomorrow, the first of June.

Inside, I have lighted the usual driftwood fire. Enough driftwood collects on the shores of this island to build a roof over Scotland, and some is from North America. It makes a good glow, and in a bedroom grate it is something to stare into before sleep – an illusion of warmth before the cold of the night. Some recent days have been so fair that we have gone to the beaches, but the indoor temperature is forty-two at the moment. Donald Gibbie said a couple of things tonight that are now, somehow, there in the fire. He and Margaret invited us to their house for a dram, and that was followed by tea and pancakes. The manner in which an evening ends here is a model for the world to follow. When the Colonsay hostess feels that the day is over and there has been enough of talking, she heats the tea-kettle and opens the tin of pancakes she has prepared earlier in the day. She spreads butter on the pancakes and steeps the tea, then sets all before her guests, and when it has been consumed the visit is over: 'Good night and sleep well' – no obscurities about when things should end. Early in the evening, I had mentioned that I'd heard the laird would arrive soon, and I asked Donald if he still doffed his cap to him. He said that he could not help doing so. 'These class distinctions have to go. They're holding us back,' he said. 'But when I was a small boy, if I did not take off my cap before the laird I was severely punished by my parents for being disrespectful. It is too deep in me now for me to change, but I teach the children that it is unnecessary. Like the others, whenever I see the laird I say nothing unless he speaks to me. If he says something, I remove my cap and say, "Good morning, Milord", or "Good evening, Milord". I simply can't help it.' Later in the evening, Donald told me what he and the other islanders thought would happen in the event of a thermo nuclear war. What led to this was that he had been asking me for details of New York, and I told him that we had once had an apartment there in an unintelligibly large housing complex where thirty-two thousand people lived on seventy-five acres of Manhattan. Merely around our own elevator shaft – twelve floors, eight apartments per floor – lived three times the population of Colonsay. This brought the bomb to mind, because we had lived in that apartment during an era of nuclear crisis, and I told Donald and Margaret how we had expected from moment to moment that in the next instant we would be vapour, and how sometimes we would look out the window at the city at night and wonder if it would be gone by morning. Donald reacted without surprise and told me about Benbecula. There is, he said, a rocket range on Benbecula, which is one of the Hebrides, a hundred miles north-northwest of Colonsay. It is apparently not a missile installation – just a target range for small rockets. Nonetheless, almost since the beginning of the era of the hydrogen bomb the people of Colonsay have felt themselves to be living in the greatest of danger because of their proximity to Benbecula. Donald said, 'If the bomb ever does come, we shall be among the first to go.'

It is said on Colonsay that if you sneeze in Balnahard people will hear moments later in Machrins that you have pneumonia, and soon in Oronsay that you are dead. Nothing electronic has yet been developed that could outmode the gossip circuitry of this small island. People say that twenty years ago, when the population was two hundred and fifty, the gossip was extremely intense, but now that the population is half of that the intensity has doubled, for each person's turn comes up that much more often. A good thing it is, too, for not the least of the results is sanity. There is apparently a point at which gossip can become so intensely commonplace that it is not only beyond hurting anyone but is, in fact, a release.

'There is no mental illness on the island,' the doctor said to me yesterday.

'I think they're all mentally ill,' said the doctor's wife.

'Not from a medical standpoint,' the doctor said. 'You'll never kill them with quietness.'

Sometimes eruptions are direct and brief. Two men were drinking side by side last night in the pub.

'I know you think I'm a bastard,' said one, touching his cap.

The other said, 'We'll let that pass. I've not come here to discuss that.'

'I think it's time we buried the hatchet.'

'Yes, and if I had one I'd bury it in your bloody head.'

These face-to-face salutes are merely an intimation of what is said behind people's backs. In a sense, every house, hill, barn, and byre is a centre of gossip, but there are several principal ones – The Shop, the Post Office, the potting shed at Kiloran Farm, and, above all others, the pub, which has no name and is in the rear of the inn in Scalasaig. What is said in these places will frequently include a high proportion of factual incorrectness, but truth and fiction often seem to be riding the same sentence in such a way that the one would be lonely without the other. A word or two will be said about almost everyone – 'What Davidson fails to understand is that he is a foreigner here' – but far in excess of all competition the predominant subject of conversation is the laird, owner of the people's houses, owner of the land they work. The laird is a point of focus, a determining presence, the godhead of a small religion. The laird is a young man with a large family, an advanced sense of humour, and preoccupations with places other than Colonsay, but to the people of the island, where he spends his summers, he is the enigmatic embodiment of good and evil, hope and fear, keeper of the gate of Heaven and Hell, fate's own fulcrum, overlord, landlord.

It is 10 p.m. and, in the pub, time to drink up. A notice on the wall says, 'Under the provisions of the Licencing Act, 1961, a period of ten minutes is allowed at the end of the morning and evening periods of permitted hours for the consumption of alcoholic liquors purchased during such hours. It is an offence for customers to consume alcoholic liquors after this ten-minute period. Maximum penalty £100.'

'Ten minutes, gentlemen.'

'The laird is an evil man in several senses of the word.'

'As a boy, he took his sweets off and ate them by himself in the woods.'

'That, I should say, is characteristic of him today.'

'His two brothers and his sister – they shared sweets with others.'

'His father had more money than he has, but once you get past the third million, what's money?'

'His grandmother had seven million.'

'In her day, the money was still new. The first Baron Strathcona, the laird's great-grandfather, was nothing more than an Aberdeenshire crofter's son – a herd laddie in his tartan rags looking over the cows. He went to Canada and sold firearms to the Indians – the old matchlock rifles – and he got skins for the rifles.'

'And for the skins he got Colonsay, the finest island in the whole Hebrides.'

'The finest island in the whole Hebrides to get the bloody hell out of.'

Overhead, nailed high on a wall, is a giant lobster claw, at least ten inches long. A sign behind the bar says, 'Weights and Measures Act, 1963. Gin, rum, vodka, and whisky are offered in quantities of $\frac{1}{5}$ of a gill or multiples thereof.'

'The laird has no time for islanders. His father's attitude towards us was one of slight contempt. This one, I think, really hates our guts.'

'I remember him saying once, "When Daddy dies, things will change drastically." I never forgot it.'

'If the old laird had lived forever, things would have been all right.'

'The new one says he is losing money. I have no idea where. He spends none on the island.'

'He spent forty thousand pounds to restore his house in Bath.'

70

'Och, it was a hundred and twenty thousand. That's why he lets the island go to subsistence sums.'

'He is the chairman of the Bath Festival. He has no time for Colonsay.'

'He doesn't have the money you think he has. There were death duties, you know.'

'There are ways to circumvent them.'

'The old laird's estate was only worth three hundred and sixty thousand pounds.'

'Och, three million six hundred thousand would be more like it.'

'The laird is a Lloyd's underwriter, and to be that you have to put down at least five hundred thousand.'

'The old laird loved the wild geese, the greylag geese. Thousands of them stop here. He hoped they would breed here. No one dared to shoot a wild goose. The old laird would go around at night saying, "Did you hear a shot?" '

'The old laird himself was a good shot.'

'The new laird doesn't do much in the way of shooting. He's not a good shot. Before Calum the Gamekeeper became redundant, they were out shooting at snipes, and the laird kept missing, and he complained to Calum – "I'm not hitting anything," he said. And Calum said, "And I don't think you will, Milord, until you start using both barrels. The shells only cost eightpence apiece." '

'Mean, parsimonious, close-fisted is the laird.'

'He's a great yachtsman.'

'A *very good* yachtsman.'

'Seventy-five per cent of the time he's on the island is spent mucking about in his boat.'

'When he goes to Kiloran Bay, if there's three people on the beach he calls it Blackpool.'

'He thinks he's the cat's pajamas.'

'He's a very vain man.'

71

'Mind you, he's a broth of a boy.'

'A blue-eyed boy.'

'Lady Strathcona is of Norman aristocracy – well diluted, I believe.'

'Her grandmother was a housemaid.'

'She is of penurious stock, blue-blooded but not moneyed.'

'And what have they done for the island? They have erected a sheep fank, and they have repaired two fences.'

'They've let it seep out that the island can bloody well fend for itself.'

'The factor has spread it around.'

'Redundancies.'

'People are in panic stations.'

'Drink up, please.'

'People complained about the old laird, too. Let us not forget that. They said he did what he pleased. Why shouldn't he do what he pleased? He was paying for it.'

'This one isn't paying for it.'

'His father spoiled the people of this island. He didn't want industry. He wanted the island unspoiled. When people were out of work, he took them on at the estate and paid them for doing damn all.'

'Quite frankly, when this laird took over it was too late.'

'People have been depending too much on Lord Strathcona. We have lost our sense of independence. There is too much soft living – National Health, Unemployment. You get money for sitting on your backside. It all adds up to a loss of independence.'

'Lord Strathcona is a trained economist. The factor is one of the ablest factors in Scotland. We tenants sometimes—'

'The estate had two factors for a long time. I feel

sorry for a laird who has not got enough sense to have one factor instead of two.'

'There is where the money is pouring out. If the laird wants to save money, he should get rid of the other factor as well.'

'We tenants sometimes have a biased view of it all. The economic problem is people. If you get rid of people – all kinds of people – you are three-quarters of the way to solving the problem. More money is going out than is coming in. They have to get rid of the human problem – use professional labour instead of salary labour. Strathcona has done nothing diabolical. He has just got rid of the human problem.'

'He's a feudal lord. You must remember that. He has responsibilities.'

'Good night.'

'Good night.'

'Sleep well.'

'Bye-bye just now.'

If the people's favourite dartboard is the laird, their second choice is the factor. There is, of course, a powerful tradition in the Highlands of odium toward factors, and Colonsay, since time out of memory, has not been an exception. Some years after the murder of the last Colonsay chief, there was a period when the Campbells controlled the island, from their castle in Inveraray. They sent a factor to Colonsay whose name was Donald MacEwan but who swiftly became known as Spotted Donald. As factors went, Spotted Donald was particularly cruel, and when, finally, he expropriated the only cow of a poor widow, certain men of the island went to his house, tore him away from a dinner of seal meat and potatoes, dragged him to Balaromin Mor, and put seven bullets into him as he stood tied to the same standing stone where the last chief had perished. Word was forwarded to Inveraray that if another factor like

Spotted Donald was sent to the island the same thing would happen.

In another era, there was a factor on Colonsay who was known as Grey Samuel the Lecher. Surrounded by women whom he attracted through his fiscal powers, he lived in Dun Ghallain, a fortress on a high promontory over the waves at the western edge of Machrins. When he abused the island clansmen one time too many, they castrated him. Later, he was killed by accident when the roof of his house fell in, and a cairn – Grey Samuel's Cairn – now marks the site, by Foul Harbour. Seven hundred yards off Oronsay is an islet called Eilean Ghaoidmeal (the Island That Stole the Rent), and the story behind the name is that a factor once embezzled money and buried it there, but the money was never found, by him or by anyone else.

Tommy Findlay, of modern times and lately made redundant, was a friend of Andrew Oronsay. Findlay the Factor and Andrew Oronsay were once rival skippers in the annual sailing regatta, which is now defunct for lack of interest, but competition – between two-man sailing dinghies – used to be fierce. Andrew was a very good yachtsman, and before one regatta he acquired a new dinghy in order to favour his bid for the championship. Findlay the Factor sailed the laird's dinghy. Full of zeal, he carried too much sail, and in the course of the race tipped over. His crewman was Peter Bella. Standing on the shore, Peter Bella's wife, Bella Peter, screamed that Peter Bella could not swim and would drown. In order to save Peter Bella, Andrew had to lose the race, but he did not have to lose the day. Approaching the laird's dinghy, he found Findlay in the water hanging on admirably to the waist of the thrashing Peter. Cautiously and without hurry, he soothed Peter Bella with his voice and gradually hauled him to safety in his dinghy. By now, Findlay the Factor was so exhausted that he had trouble moving and could not pull himself out of the water. There had been other times when Andrew had had Findlay in a tight position. Andrew, so the story goes, had once invited Findlay to Oronsay for a week-end, and had put him in a room where the roof leaked, and Findlay had got soaked during the night. But Findlay had nonetheless neglected to have the roof fixed, and now, as he bobbed in the water, calling, 'Haul me out, haul me out,' Andrew seized him and pushed him under. Pulling him up into the air, Andrew said, 'And when are you going to fix the slates on my roof?' There being no immediate answer, Andrew returned Findlay to the sub-surface. Pulling him up again, Andrew said, 'When? Now? This week?' and when Findlay nodded Andrew pulled him out. Findlay the Factor once expressed the belief that although incomers run the economy of the island, the island really belongs to the islanders – an ultimate insight if ever there was one, and that is exactly what it proved to be for Findlay, who was eventually made redundant, and left the island.

A third of all the rental income derived by the laird from the crofts, farms, and other properties of Colonsay goes to pay the salary of David Wardhaugh, the present factor. Wardhaugh lives in Forfar, in County Angus, and each month when the time for Rent Day approaches, he drives across the breadth of Scotland, through Strathmore and Strath Earn and on through Argyll, riding the Lochiel out to Colonsay, where he collects rents, listens to complaints, and tends the flame of the feudal system. Inevitably known as the Wart Hog, Wardhaugh does not deserve such facile opprobrium, for he is apparently an empathetic man, endowed with a strong awareness of the history of his line of work in Scotland and a desire to be as just as he must be realistic. His mission is plain enough. The laird simply has no wish to be the animated exchequer of an insular, private, picayune welfare state – or, to give the situation its full setting, a welfare state within a welfare state. The factor makes recommendations on the revision of rents and the renewal of leases and, particularly, on the creation of redundancies, and he sooner or later provokes hostility in almost every part of the island. He has the personal advantage of not being resident on Colonsay, and when he is present he keeps to himself at Colonsay House, the laird's place, in Kiloran, eating his meals alone and retiring early. He is a heavy set man with thinning hair and a manner of rumpled tweed – pleasant, practical, somewhat didactic. He knows an anachronism when he sees one, even in a mirror. Of both the actions and the responsibilities of the laird, he says, 'Lord Strathcona is doing what the government *should* be doing.'

Rent Day approaches now, and this time both the factor and the laird are on the island. The people, nostalgic for anything having to do with the old laird, are particularly nostalgic for Rent Day as it was when he was alive. The old laird and Findlay the Factor used to sit at a table in the inn, and as each tenant – each crofter, cotter, farmer – came to the table with his money, the laird would say, 'And how *are* you?'

'Very well,' said the tenant. 'Very well, thank you, Milord.'

'You're looking fit,' said the laird.

'Thank you, Milord.'

'Very fit indeed.'

Then the tenant would in all likelihood proceed to give the laird news of a broken window, a leaking roof, a stovepipe disengaged. The old laird never argued. All complaints went into Findlay's notebook, for attention. After any request at all, the laird would say, 'Right. Findlay, you look into that.' And a month or six later the tenant would say, 'Milord, about that stovepipe . . .' And the laird would say, 'Findlay, why have you not done anything about it?' And Findlay would make another note in his book.

Why these times are remembered with nostalgia is obscure, but in part it is because of the genteel and graceful manner with which the laird always brought off the scene, and in part because he had on the table a bottle of sherry and a bottle of whisky. All who came to pay had their choice of drinks when they had done so. 'Rent Day was a good day, a social day,' one tenant – the storekeeper, Alistair Allan – said, describing it to me. 'You took your glass and you rose and said, "My respects, Milord," and you drank your whisky – "a drop of himself", as Skye men say.' When all had paid their rents and had their drams, they left the inn together and went round the island, stopping at each house for a few more drops of himself. Everyone got pretty full, as an islander would put it, and Rent Day, always a Saturday, finally ended at about five o'clock Sunday morning.

There is much less drinking now, in the new era of austerity, and Rent Day is held at the estate office in Colonsay House. I have asked a considerable number of islanders if they intend to be there this time, and almost to a man they have said, 'Och, no, I can't be bothered, I can't be bothered, I'll just mail in a cheque and be done with it' – or some close variation of that theme. The hour has come, however, and in the courtyard at the side of Colonsay House they are all present. To a man, they are impeccably dressed. They wear ties. The hair of some is wet from brushing. Their cheeks shine. In appearance, they are a church congregation, but in number they are more than the minister is accustomed to seeing. Donald Gibbie. Donald Garvard. Andrew Oronsay. There are no absentees. One by one, cap in hand, they go in to see the laird.

'Good morning, Milord.'

The laird is younger than nearly all the men who have

come to pay him their money and their respects. He is good-looking, tall, athletic, a bit heavy in the cheek, with long swept-back straight hair, amusement in his eyes, and the accents of Eton and Cambridge in his voice.

'And how *are* you?' he asks. 'You're looking fit.'

'Thank you, Milord.'

'Fit indeed.'

'Milord, I thought I might mention that I have a fence down, and . . .'

'Wardhaugh, make a note of that.'

———————————

I have volunteered to help the laird prepare his launch for use by a group of marine biologists from the University of Glasgow and the British Museum. In earlier explorations, the scientists have discovered beneath the waters off Colonsay the largest laminaria forest they have ever seen – sequoias of seaweed so dense that men can move among them only in single file along the bottom of the sea. Within these forests they have found a tiny red alga of a type previously seen only in the waters of California, and today, as soon as the launch is ready, they will return to the rubbery wilderness to renew and perhaps to expand their discoveries. The air temperature at the moment is forty-two degrees and the water temperature is exactly the same. There is a strong wind. The sea is choppy. The biologists are up in the inn checking over their equipment – underwater cameras, lanterns, wet-suits – and the laird is in the open-sided shed at the edge of Port na Feamainn (Seaweed Harbour), where his launch has been wedged in storage through the winter. He wears a baggy and partly shredded crimson pullover, tattered plus-fours, and frayed leather shoes that are covered with worms of dried paint. He is assisted by Dougie McGilvray, an unredundant hand from the home farm, and Dougie has with him a tractor, which he is manoeuvering into position between the shed and the water. The launch is perhaps twenty-five feet long, has a large rust-covered inboard engine, and appears to be planted in the shed, an inertia of tons. It is unimaginable that a tractor of the size of Dougie's could ever pull it out of there. The laird collects bruised and rotting timbers for use as impromptu rollers. He kicks props away from the gunwales of the launch. He pauses and points out a dory just up the beach – one of his dories – that has a staved-in hull plank. 'That's the sort of thing that bothers this particular laird,' he says. 'The boat was left in the open, and that is what happened.' When it is repaired, the laird is the one who will do the job. All his life – that is, during all his summers from boyhood, here on Colonsay – he has been a fixer and builder of boats. He is a general carpenter as well. He repairs the furniture in Colonsay House. He describes himself as 'an artisan *manqué*'. Two or three nights ago, after a dinner of sherried broth, mutton, and several bottles of Burgundy, he showed me, in a roomful of tools and planking, the boat he is working on at the moment – a sailing dinghy. While he talked, he picked up a chisel and shaved away lightly at its bowpiece and gunwales. As he worked, he said, among other things, 'I love this place, and in a few years, when the children are older, I want to come live here, and I also want to die here.' Now, by Seaweed Harbour, it is beginning to rain, and the rain is ice-cold. The tide is low and turning. Dougie has the tractor in position, and the laird loops a sorry-looking rope between the tractor and the launch, which will emerge, if at all, stern first. One of the scientists approaches along the shore, wearing boots, denim trousers, a black slicker. 'I'm terribly sorry, but I shan't be able to introduce you to this chap,' the laird says. 'I've forgotten his name.' The arriving figure turns out to be a woman. She is a distinguished don. The other marine biologists, whose ages vary widely, join us as well. Several young men are in wet-suits and ready to dive. The whole sea-weed team is impatient. The tractor roars, and lunges toward the water. The launch moves, its rudder bracket cutting down into the sand and heavy gravels of the shore. The rudder bracket is nearly rusted through, so this essentially clumsy operation has got to be delicate. The laird, with strength surprising even for a man his size, rams a plank into the gravel and under the keel of the launch, and pries up the stern, while the rest of us stuff the impromptu rollers into place. The tractor erupts again, and the launch moves another foot. The laird pries it up. The rain is coming down hard, and on the wind it is coming at an angle that stings. Fifteen minutes go by, and now the tractor is so close to the water that it is useless. Dougie removes it. Everyone heaves at the gunwales to move the launch farther. 'We should avoid going in to the left there, if we can,' the laird says. 'They sort of blew up some rocks here once, to deepen the harbour. That area is full of primordial ooze.' Finally, the launch rests on props in shallow water. The incoming tide will float it. The biologists load up, and the laird miraculously starts the rusted engine. But there is a hole in the exhaust. The laird goes off to a small building on the harbourside where he keeps naut-ical supplies. The place is full of oarlocks, anchors, paints, ropes. He rummages for a Jubilee clip – an adjustable steel band secured by a screw – and while he does so he confides to me that his appreciation of the spirit of scientific inquiry has made him feel not entirely comfortable about the fact that he is renting the launch to the scientists for an attractive price. The clip he finds is rusty, but it will do. Back on the beach, the seaweed people are standing around restlessly, smoking. They wanted to get going an hour ago. Sitting in the launch with rain driving horizontally into his face, his long hair hanging down in strings all about his head, the laird bears down on the Jubilee clip's screw. He says, 'This screw hasn't moved since God was a boy.' The screw-driver slips, and its point goes into and almost through a finger of his left hand. Blood wells up and runs across his fingers and the palm of his hand, mixing with rain and diesel oil. 'There I go, trying to screw myself instead of the boat,' he says. After much effort, he tightens the clip. The engine is covered with gore. The diving team and its surface dons are ready to go. As the tide washes up around them, the laird keeps handing them small pieces of frayed rope and used hardware that might serve well in an emergency. The laird's right hand is almost as red from cold as his left hand is with blood. It is still raining. The launch begins to move under power. 'Goodbye,' the laird calls. 'I admire you more than I can possibly say. The thought of diving today fills me with the utmost gloom.'

There is a graveyard just in front of Donald Gibbie's croft, in Kilchattan, and this for many years has been the island's main burial ground. On a low, flat, and unadorn-ed tombstone beside the graveyard's southern wall are the words 'Donald Third Baron Strathcona and Mount Royal, 1891–1959.' He was the old laird, and the only laird in modern times to be buried on Colonsay. It was, of course, his wish. His mother, who held the title before him, and his grandfather, the First Baron Strathcona and Mount Royal, had not really been much in evidence on the island they owned. But the old laird apparently looked upon solitude as a form of capital, and the larg-est share of it he had in his life was on Colonsay. He was a tall, spare man. Alone, he would go to the coastline of uninhabited Balavetchy, where he built with his own hands over a period of years a stone pier for small boats of the type that his oldest son, Euan, was forever making and sailing. 'The island had been a place where the family went for a long picnic once a year,' Euan now says. 'My father increasingly regarded it as his home. Nearly all my boyhood recollections are here. We came here, absolutely always, for the summer. I bathed like a maniac in all weather, made boats, sailed, shot grouse.' Euan, who would eventually wonder if the twentieth century could ever completely reach Colonsay, meanwhile watched its tentative approaches: the first telephone, in 1940; the first automobile, in 1947; electricity, in 1952.

Euan was born in 1923, in London. After his Eton years and one year at Trinity College, Cambridge, he went to McGill University, in Montreal, where he earned a degree in engineering. He is a director of various small manufacturing companies, the chief of which is Tallon Ltd, a maker of ballpoint pens, and before his life was altered by the death of his father and his own accession to the peerage, he was an employee, for seven years, of Urwick, Orr & Partners Ltd, a management-consulting firm in Newcastle, for which he specialized in lavatory valves, foundation garments, and oil seals. Now in Bath he lives in an attractive but unprepossessing segment of an eighteenth-century crescent that he helped to restore. His wife, whom he married in 1954, is a daughter of the Twelfth Earl Waldegrave. Her name is Jinny, and she is pretty and quick, slim, dark-haired, girlish, bright-eyed. She has a wash of freckles. She is the manager of the Schola Cantorum, the university choir of Oxford. She helps her husband with his chairmanship of the annual Bath Festival and looks after their six children, the youngest of whom – Emma and Andrew – are twins. Her capacity for nonchalance seems about equal to the laird's. 'Both of us take the peerage business quite lightly,' she said one evening. 'Euan has no strong atavistic feelings as a laird. He is not the traditional, native, Scottish laird. His great-grandfather was a Scot, but he is English, and even among his Eton-Cambridge friends he is most untypical. He has done things they would consider unthinkable. He went to McGill, and, worse, during the war he went into the Navy and ignored the Guards.'

'I drove a motor torpedo boat with singular lack of distinction,' said the laird.

She said, 'You were wounded in the bottom, darling.'

On his mother's side, the laird is descended not only from Jeremiah Colman, the mustard king, but also from Nell Gwyn, the orange wench. During the Restoration, young women carrying baskets of oranges used to stand near the stage in London theatres, face the audience, and sell oranges at sixpence apiece and themselves for a little more. The girls were known as Orange Girls, and they worked under the administration of women called Orange Molls. Nell Gwyn, a beautiful and illiterate Orange Girl, became a minor actress and the mistress of King Charles II. 'Anybody may know she has been an orange wench by her swearing,' said the Duchess of Portsmouth. Nell Gwyn died when she was thirty-seven, but she lived to see her son made Duke of St Albans. 'My mother's line included the bluest of illegitimate blue-bloods – the Duke of St Albans,' the laird has told me. On his father's side, the laird is descended from North American Indians. One of his great-great-grand-mothers was a full-blooded Cree. His great-grandfather Donald Smith, of Forres, Morayshire, Scotland, married a half-Indian girl in the Canadian wilderness, perform-ing the ceremony himself, in the absolute absence of clergy. Smith, who would become the First Baron Strathcona and Mount Royal, was, in the words of a biographer, a child of parents 'by no means greatly blessed with this world's goods' – the second son of a village merchant. He grew up in a house that resembled, in its essentials, the houses of the crofters of Colonsay and of the Highlands in general. He went to a school that had been established for children of 'necessitous parents', and when he was eighteen he signed on as a clerk with the Hudson's Bay Company and was sent to a trading post on the St Lawrence River. He spent five years there and fifteen more in Labrador, and rose from clerk to trader to chief trader to chief factor to chief executive officer of the Hudson's Bay Company in Canada, headquartered in Montreal. In time, he became High Commissioner for Canada and, as a member of the Canadian Parliament, author of the Smith Liquor act, which prohibited the sale and use of alcoholic drinks in the Northwest Territories. To help enforce the act, he wrote the recommendation that resulted in the creation of the Northwest Mounted Police. He also became a founding director of the Canadian Pacific. By his colleagues' acknowledgment, it was largely through his perseverance that the great railway was completed across the Rockies. He was by now the richest man in Canada. White beard flowing, he drove the final spike – at Craigellachie, in British Columbia, November 7, 1885. The spike is now on Colonsay, in a small showcase in the laird's house, and there is a groove in it where iron has been removed so that bits of the spike could be set among the diamonds in the brooches of various Strathcona women. On a wall close by is the family crest and coat of arms. The heraldry – 'gules, on a fesse argent . . .' – includes a demi-lion rampant over a hammer and spike, four men paddling a canoe, a beaver gnawing a maple tree, and, over all, the Strathcona motto: 'Perseverance'.

Showing me all this one day, the laird said that his great-grandfather, after a time as chancellor of McGill

University, had returned to Britain as a representative of
Canada. 'Home with his fortune, he sort of thought the
time had come for an estate and a peerage,' the laird went
on. 'So he bought Glencoe.' Anciently a MacDonald
territory and the scene of the worst massacre in the era of
the clans, Glencoe became the seat of the family until
1930, when it was sold. Meanwhile, Queen Victoria had
obliged with the peerage, and Donald Smith became, in
full title, Baron Strathcona and Mount Royal of Glencoe
in the County of Argyll and Montreal in the Province of
Quebec. 'Strathcona' was mere linguistic prestidigitation
– another way of saying 'Glencoe'. Colonsay was acquired
as a kind of afterthought. Smith had loaned some money
to the last McNeill laird of Colonsay, and when McNeill
died, Smith gave an additional sum to McNeill's heirs and
took over the island, for an aggregate of forty-four
thousand pounds. The first Lord Strathcona's only child
was a daughter, and through something called a 'special
remainder', cordially dispensed by the Crown, permission was granted that his title pass to her. Thus the second
Baron was a woman. Her husband, R. J. B. Howard, was a
Canadian physician. Their grandson Euan Howard is the
Fourth Baron Strathcona and Mount Royal, and Colonsay's present laird.

The laird, with his legs stretched out, is sitting, sipping
whisky, on a low bench before a log fire at Colonsay
House in late evening, his wife beside him. He has been
considering, with only minor signs of emotion, the fact
that he is the least popular man on the island he owns. He
accepts this as inevitable, if not pleasant. He is sorry, but
he cannot accept the anachronism he stepped into when
he became laird in 1959. It is an odd summer place
indeed that includes one hundred and thirty-eight
dependent people. Embalmed in law, the crofting system
of the Highlands is borne forward ever more incongruously toward the twenty-first century, perfectly

protecting people from the terrors of the eighteenth century while isolating them from the twentieth. One crofter pays the laird six pounds rent a year, another forty pounds; the average is fifteen pounds. 'Rents here at the moment are lower than they were in 1905. The Depression pushed them down. Rent is fixed by the Scottish Land Court, which will add a pound or two in rent for thousands in improvements.' One cotter lives free, another pays five pounds a year, another pays seven pounds. Their houses could be rented to summer people for fifty pounds. Houses that were put up for thirty-five hundred pounds rent for fifteen pounds a year. The whole of Machrins farm – three thousand acres and two houses, one of which has nine bedrooms – rents for four hundred pounds a year. Neil Darroch said his chimney was smoking and asked for a cowl. A cowl would cost fifty-five shillings. Darroch's annual rent is less than that. 'When I inherited, the estate was losing more than ten thousand pounds a year. The rent income was two thousand pounds and we were spending well above twelve thousand pounds around the island, and that does not include money spent on our own house and gardens. The people regarded it as axiomatic that we would provide work. Finally, in 1965, we said, "To hell with all this," and began creating redundancies, applying for increases in rents, not replacing people who retired or died. We have given the electrical generator plants to the people to run and maintain. It's actually a permanent, interest-free loan. If anyone is going to sell the generators and have a wild weekend in Glasgow, I want it to be me. We used to have a gamekeeper and a forestry staff, but we've packed that up for the moment. Now we are close to washing our face, but it's been at the sacrifice of the economic balance of the island. I blame my own family for getting the people into the situation they are in now. My father's benevolence was misplaced. It is not easy, or practical, to maintain a paradise. People complain about broken skylights and let the rain pour into their houses while they wait for the estate to repair the damage. Waiting for the estate, they leave windows unpainted, and the windows rot out. For sixty years, these people have never been made to do repairs which legitimately belong to them. One wants to educate them to have enough pride to stand on their own feet. They've got to put their fair share into the pot. Donald Gibbie would be a bad example, because from what you tell me he has got the message already. Most of the people here are very lazy, and they are two-faced, in a nice way. They have great charm. They're happy-go-lucky. They're well educated. They always like to give you the answer you want to hear. This sometimes makes them seem to be downright liars, which they are; I would ask you to bear this in mind. Colonsay has an ancient feudal society which basically wants to go on being feudal, provided they can find someone who wants to play at – and finance – being a feudal baron. The term "laird" is slightly fey and old-fashioned. I am the landlord and the proprietor. These are the facts. I let houses to the other people. The island is my property. All the people live in houses that belong to me. It's a perfectly modern contractual situation. Offhand, I can't think of any ancient rights which are vested in the owner of Colonsay. The paternalistic and benevolent landlord cannot go on being as paternalistic and benevolent as he used to be, and this calls into question the viability of the whole community. The curious thing about our situation is that it is happening on an island. If I lived in Fort William and had to make the odd man redundant, he could find work nearby. My position here would be even more of an incongruity than it is were it not based on a deep tradition. The tradition, however, is becoming less and less tenable. It's frightfully tempting to say, "To hell with these bloody idle so-and-sos", but one must remember that for sixty years they have been cosseted. They are entitled to be a little sore when they are dragged screaming into the twentieth century. It's a dicey business for *me!*'

Wherever the laird goes, whether he is hauling a boat out of Loch a' Sgoltaire or walking along Kiloran Bay, he is surrounded by his jumping, nattering, extroverted children. He and his wife walk in the deep parallel ruts of the long driveway to Colonsay House, each holding one of Andrew's hands and swinging the little boy high in the air with every second stride. The laird and his wife have many times stayed up until three in the morning, painting, sweeping, glazing if necessary, to get cottages ready for summer rentals. Their daughter Caroline, who is eight years old, has been living with a housekeeper here for several months now, so that she can go to the island school. Down by the harbour in Scalasaig is a strange shack that consists of four impromptu walls and a vaulted roof that is actually an overturned dory. The laird built it when he was young. The inverted dory is in the most public place on the island and serves, to my eye, at least, as a kind of reminder that when it comes to building codes or zoning, on whatever level, the whole zone is the laird's. Kiloran, the area he generally keeps to, is as different from the rest of the island as the laird is from its people. The vale of Kiloran is completely surrounded by high hills, which interrupt the winds from all directions. On an island that is assaulted by the storms of the North Atlantic, Kiloran is a glen of privileged protection, and it is so lush that people travel from other continents to see it. The earlier Strathcona lairds developed gardens in Kiloran that are among the best in the west of Scotland, known mainly for their profusions of rhododendron. Palm trees were introduced there long ago (the air temperature seldom goes below forty), and they are tall and healthy, growing beside Colonsay House. The house was built in 1722, on the site of the graveyard of an abbey that once stood in Kiloran. Human bones sometimes surface in the gardens. Once French Provincial and symmetrical, the building has been given so many additions that it is now miscellaneous. It has twenty bedrooms, each with a name painted on its door – Balnahard, Garvard, Balaromin Mor – and a billiard room and a library, all high-ceilinged and musty and cavernous. Edward VII came to Kiloran and planted a tree. The Britannia dropped anchor in Kiloran Bay several years ago and the present Royal Family had a picnic there with the laird and his family. When the Queen has a picnic, she brings her own food. The laird was her guest for lunch. She had come to see Kiloran Bay, three-quarters of a mile of gold-white crescent sand, said to be the finest beach in the Hebrides. Once a year, a chartered cruise ship, dazzling white from bow to stern, stops at Colonsay so that members of the National Trust for Scotland can see the island for themselves. The ship has too deep a draught for the pier. Sailors bring the passengers ashore in power launches, and most of the men aboard are dressed in great blazing kilts, and the women wear tartan bonnets and assertive tartan skirts. The laird is there to greet them. He wears the baggiest tweed suit in the United Kingdom, with plus fours and a waistcoat, and on his feet are old, weather-beaten shoes. The suit, resplendently frayed, nobly tattered, appears to have been cut in 1905. He cleans his pipe and spills dottle all over his waistcoat. The dottle blends with several generations of ash already there. He appears to be cheerfully resigned to being an exhibit of the Hebrides. Somehow, he has not compromised. He is pure Sassenach and all laird.

One night about sixty years ago, my grandmother and grandfather were awakened by the steady howling of a dog.

My grandmother touched my grandfather's shoulder and said to him in a frightened voice, 'Oh, Angus, listen, that is a sign of death.' Jumping out of bed, Angus said, 'You're damned right it is – if that dog is still there when I get down the stairs and out the door.' If events fade into legend and legend into superstition, superstition eventually fades away altogether, and it is impossible to say how that one made its way to my grandmother in Ohio; but if it came from Colonsay one certainty now is that it has long since vanished from the island. Legend hangs above the Hebrides more thickly than clouds, but the people pay even less attention to these things – to haunted dogs, seal women, seers, mermaids, elves, fairies, glaistigs, gigelorums – than they do to the rain. Donald Gibbie believes in nothing supernatural, and he says he knows few people who do. Donald Gibbie spends his time worrying about, among other things, the Common Market and 'what effect Great Britain's entry into it might have on subsidies as we know them'. It is not the islanders who preserve the early magic of the island. It is the women who stay at the inn – the ones with the knitted caps and tweed skirts and walking sticks, some of whom have brought their own shepherd's crooks with them from Edinburgh. At home in Midlothian, they belong to organizations like the Highland Hall Association and the Edinburgh Gaelic Circle, and they go to regular meetings where, in effect, they burn tartan candles. In their heads hang splendid tapestries of Hebridean lore and legend, and when they come to the island, for their brief visits of a week or ten days, they become solitary silhouettes in the heather on the hilltops, drinking in the air of ages past and imagining themselves to be in the company of forms unseen. They themselves are inconspicuous – Donald Gibbie says he sees them only when they get off the Lochiel and again when they get back on – and they are sometimes unexpected. Two or three days ago, a fine-tweed lady with powdered hair and a varnished crook jumped out from behind a whin bush, tugged my sleeve, and told me not to kiss a fairy or I might never see the human world again. These women know the history of the island. On the moorlands of Balaromin Mor, one of them asked my name, and when I told her she said, 'I thought as you approached that I was seeing a ghost, and now I know that a ghost is what I see. What is your Christian name?'

'John.'

'Have you another name?'

'Yes, I do.'

'What is that?'

'Angus.'

'The Cross of Christ be upon us.'

This woman, who introduced herself as a Jardine of Applegirth, told me that she believed she had second sight, and suspected that I had it, too. Second sight is one of the immemorial talents of the Highlands. People of Colonsay are said to have possessed it, but none was ever particularly noted for it. The greatest man of all time in this field was Kenneth Mackenzie, the Brahan Seer, beside whom Nostradamus, a near contemporary, should have paled into French insignificance. Mackenzie was a farm worker in what is now Ross and Cromarty. In a later day, he might have been a crofter. Word of his power spread when he began predicting with accuracy not only certain deaths and other local events but also the birth of a child with two navels and another with four thumbs. Soon, he began to travel the Highlands telling the future. He said that ships would one day sail behind Tomnahurich Hill, in Inverness, predicting, a hundred and fifty years before its construction, the Caledonian Canal. Walking on Culloden Moor, a hundred years before the clans were destroyed there, he said, 'This bleak moor shall, before many generations have passed away, be stained with the best blood of the High-lands. Glad am I that I will not see that day, for it will be a fearful period. Heads will be cut off by the score, and no mercy will be shown or quarter given on either side.' He also said, on another occasion, 'The clans will flee their native country before an army of sheep.' A third prophecy in this progression has not yet been fulfilled. The Brahan Seer said that eventually even the sheep would be gone and 'the whole country will be so utterly desolated and depopulated that the crow of a cock shall not be heard north of Druim-Uachdair ... The deer and other wild animals in the huge wilderness shall be exterminated by horrid black rains.' Mackenzie had his lighter side. He said, 'The time will come when whisky or dram shops will be so plentiful that one will be met with almost at the head of every plough furrow.' His fame became universal in the Highlands, and he a figure of importance everywhere. Donald Gibbie, with a smirk of disavowal, has given me a biography of the Seer that once belonged to his father. The Seer was apparently not only shrewd but also sarcastic, flippant, caustic, and funny, and these attributes brought about his death, after the wife of the Mackenzie chief summoned him to Brahan Castle and asked him if her husband was safe. For many months, the Mackenzie had been in Paris. 'Safe? I would *say* so,' said the Seer.

'What is he doing?'

'He is happy and merry and kissing the hand of a woman with his arm around her waist.'

This infuriated the chief's wife, who decided that the Seer had made his last guess, and Mackenzie did not soften the case against him when he looked over the highborn children playing in the castle yard and said that most of them appeared to have been sired by gillies and lackeys. Thus it was that the Brahan Seer was dropped into a barrel of boiling tar. Knives had been driven into the sides of the barrel. He said a word or two before he went. He said, 'I see into the far future, and I read the doom of the race of my oppressor, whose long-descended line will, before many generations have passed, end in extinction and in sorrow. I see a chief, the last of his house, both deaf and dumb. He will be the father of four fair sons, all of whom he will follow to the tomb. He will live careworn and die mourning, knowing that the honours of his line are to be extinguished forever, and that no future chief of the Mackenzie shall rule at Brahan or in Kintail. As a sign by which it may be known that these things are coming to pass, there shall be four great lairds in the days of the last deaf-and-dumb Mackenzie chief – Gairloch, Chisholm, Grant, and Raasay – of whom one shall be buck-toothed, another hare-lipped, another half-witted, and the fourth a stammerer. When the last chief looks around him and sees them, he may know that his sons are doomed to death, that his broad lands shall pass away to the stranger, and that his race shall come to an end.' The Brahan Seer then went into the tar. Many generations later, a deaf-and-dumb Mackenzie chief came along. He had four sons. Among his contemporaries were the Chisholm of Chisholm, who was harelipped; the laird of Gairloch, who was buck-toothed; a half-witted Grant, who was a laird as well; and the stammering laird of Raasay. The four Mackenzie sons died before their father, and with him the line was extinguished forever.

Along the shores of Colonsay, and particularly of Oronsay, conical mounds rise like miniature green volcanoes. These are *sithein*, said to have been once inhabited by a race of *sith* (little people), who wore conical green caps, green coats, and green kilts. These little people bracketed the world with good and evil, extending benevolence to ordinary humans who treated them well and devising unhappiness for people who treated them badly. Things left beside their hillocks for mending or repairing would be taken care of in the night. They knew cures for diseases. They played small bagpipes, and they ate silverweed and heather. Their women could assume the shape of deer. They made love to human beings, and, perhaps not surprisingly, they were more faithful to their lovers than their lovers were to them. They could not go below the high-water mark. They travelled in the eddy winds.

Sith (pronounced 'she') also meant 'the people of peace', 'the still folk', 'the silently moving people'. There was once no question in anyone's mind that they existed, and milk was poured into the ground to feed them. The membrane was very thin, in the islands, between the supernatural world and the physical world, and sometimes there was no discernible separation at all. History proliferated into fantasy, and pure fantasy became history. Science may erase these things, but in a sense they were true once, and they are not entirely forgotten. In the sixth century, when St Columba lived briefly on Colonsay, he was given some land in Garvard on which to build a church, so the story goes, and the result was Teampull a' Ghlinne (the Temple of the Glen), whose ruins – thick walls, arched windows – are still there, close to the boundary of Balaromin Mor. The little people frequently used to dance by the Temple of the Glen in the night, always singing a monotonous song of theirs, the complete lyrics of which were 'Sunday, Monday, Tuesday, Wednesday, Thursday, Saturday'. A hunchback from Balnahard came and joined the party one night, shouting out the lyrics with joy and carefully omitting mention of the word 'Friday', because he knew it was forbidden among the *sith*. The little people sent him back to Balnahard standing straight and humpless. Another hunchback, who lived in Kiloran, heard about this and showed up at the next dance at the temple.

'Sunday, Monday, Tuesday, Wednesday, Thursday,' sang the little people, and the Kiloran hunchback belted out a thunderstriking 'Friday'. He went home with two humps – his own and the hump of the hunchback of Balnahard. Among the *sith*, Friday was never mentioned by name. It was called the Day of Yonder Town.

Scottish surnames and the Highland clans began to evolve in the second half of the eleventh century. Many of the names had religious sources. 'MacPherson' meant 'son of the parson', 'MacTaggart' meant 'son of the priest', 'MacVicar' meant 'son of the vicar', 'Macnab' meant 'son of the abbot', 'MacLean' meant 'son of the servant of St John'. In its earliest Gaelic form, my own name – McPhee, that of Colonsay's original clan – was Mac Dubh Sith. The word '*dubh*' means 'black', and referred, in part, to the characteristically swarthy skin of these early people of the island. After they developed their tartan – of green, yellow, white, and blazing red – they added a variant sett that was simply black and white. The braid of their beginnings is not particularly obscure. A few of the green conical mounds have been opened, and within them were bone implements, stone hammers, barbed harpoons, thousands of shells, and the bones of great auks, red deer, seals, dogfish, finback whales, wild swans, sheep, rats, rabbits, boars, otters, martens, guillemots, razorbills. These were the kitchen middens of people in the Stone Age and, thereafter, of the Picts. Middens at least as extensive fill the fingery recesses of Colonsay's innumerable caves (the Piper's Cave, the Lady Cave, the Endless Cave, the Crystal Spring Cavern), where, mixed in a preserving muck, are the leavings of meals eaten by centuries of successive or concomitant tenants – by Dalriadic Scots, by Norse and Danish Vikings, and by the Celts, the Caledonian Gaels, who were known as people who endlessly asked questions, who kept larders of their dead enemies, and who described their world as *Earraghaidheal* (the Border of the Gael) and pronounced it, more or less, Argyll. With Ian Summers, an unredundant employee of the laird, I went to the Lady Cave a few days ago, at the north edge of Kiloran Bay, and set up a paraffin lantern in the absolute blackness of a tunnel offshoot that reaches back under A' Bheinn Bheag (the Little Peak), in Balnahard. The midden muck there was seemingly bottomless and was full of implements of bone and stone, and, of course, the inevitable multitude of shells. Prone in the muck, we worked systematically, following a small grid and sorting what we found. When you have in your hand the stone tine with which a man in an animal's skin ate a shellfish, the ticking of time present is incredibly accelerated. Six hours went by and the lantern was beginning to flicker after what had seemed like thirty minutes. My finger, going down in the muck just before we quit for the day, happened to go right through the centre of the circle of a bronze penannular brooch, and when I raised my hand the brooch came with it. I took it to the laird, since everything belongs to him, and he told me to keep it. He has at least a dozen such brooches in the showcase in Colonsay House with the last iron spike of the Canadian Pacific. Ancient middens are not the only middens on Colonsay. Without any apparent aesthetic conscience, the people of our own era pile their used tins and plastic bottles in pyramidal dumps near the edge of the sea, and these in time may become embedded in muck and sheathed in green.

The Vikings lived in the Hebrides for four hundred years and were there when the clans developed. The island clans were, in fact, Celto-Norse, and on Colonsay the Vikings were more numerous, proportionately, than they were on other islands. They were, in one era, followers of Magnus Bareleg, so called because when he went home he introduced the kilt to Norway, where kilts became a fad that lasted for many years. 'Havbredey', a Norse word, meant 'isle on the edge of the sea'. 'Scalasaig' and 'Uragaig' are words of Norse derivation, and 'Sgeir nan Locharnach', on the Ardskenish Peninsula, means 'the Norsemen's Skerry'. When one of the green mounds of Oronsay was opened in 1891, a Norse ship was found, and in it were the skeletons of a Viking and (*nil nisi bonum*) his wife. Viking boat burials have also been uncovered in Machrins and Kiloran Bay, but most of the green mounds are thought to have been assembled by Picts or other early peoples whose existence, transmogrified in story, underlies the legends of the *sith*. In *Popular Tales of the West Highlands* (1890), the classical work on Hebridean legend, J. F. Campbell said of the history of the *sith*, 'This class of stories is so widely spread, so matter-of-fact, hangs so well together, and is so implicitly believed that I am persuaded of the former existence of a race of men in these islands who were smaller in stature than the Celts, and who used stone arrows, lived in conical mounds, knew some mechanical arts, pilfered goods, and stole children.' Some of these small people of peace were not the most attractive beings in the world. They might have had one Cyclopean eye, or a large single nostril. The Woman of Peace, *bean shith* (the Banshee), had a huge single front tooth, preternaturally long breasts, and webbed feet. In one sitting, she could eat a cow. When a crop failed or an animal died, the still folk were said to have taken its essence, not its substance. They did steal mortal children.

> Come away, O human child!
> To the waters and the wild
> With a faery, hand in hand,
> For the world's more full of weeping
>   than you can understand.

Mrs Henry Pitney Van Dusen, wife of the retired president of Union Theological Seminary in New York, grew up as a Bartholomew, in Edinburgh, where her husband took a part of his theological training. As a young couple with infant children, the Van Dusens spent parts of several summers on Colonsay, and when I was about to leave the United States for the island, Mrs Van Dusen, who is now a neighbour of mine in Princeton, said to me, 'You must always put birch branches over a baby's cradle or baby carriage to protect it from the fairies. I did this very carefully in Colonsay.' The legends of the still folk and of related beings and phenomena have not always persisted so impressively; nor, when they have, have they very often penetrated so close to the spiritual epicentres of the modern world. Nonetheless, they seem to have grown, not to have atrophied, across the centuries. The large seeds of a treelike West Indian plant called *Entada scandens* have drifted to the shores of Colonsay for thousands of years, and they have always been called fairy eggs. People once wore them around their necks, believing that this protected them from the evil moods of fairies. Below the foundation of a new house, a cat's claws, a man's nails, a cow's hooves, and a bit of silver were traditionally buried, to keep the little people happy. Such practices and fears have pertained to all eras, ancient and modern. If a man, in more recent times, became frightened of the still folk while walking alone at night, he would draw a circle around himself and say, 'The Cross of Christ be upon me.' A troubled man in an earlier time would go, perhaps, to the summit of Ben Earrnigil, in Garvard, or to the great stones of Kilchattan, to seek reassurance from his Druid. At the summit of Ben Earrnigil is a stone circle one hundred and eight feet in diameter north to south and ninety-eight feet in diameter east to west. Stone circles in Kilchattan and elsewhere on Colonsay – and, for that matter, wherever they exist in the world – characteristically have this slight elongation, thought by some to represent the pattern of the orbit of the earth around the sun, which the Celts and their Druids worshipped. As Christians would build their cathedrals in the shape of crosses, the Celts built theirs in circles of the sun, and into the twentieth century in Argyll people used the expression 'going to the stones' when they meant 'going to church'. The Druids apparently recorded nothing. It is thought that they kept their law, philosophy, and theology in their heads, committing to memory during their period of training some sixty thousand rhymed verses, not a few of which were powerful antidotes to any threat that might rise from the still folk and the forces of the dark. The standing stones in Kilchattan, beyond the graveyard from Donald Gibbie's croft, have an abstract beauty of form and balance that has only recently been appreciated in sculpture. There are two. They stand about fifty feet apart. They are about ten feet high. What makes them so graceful is that they are quite narrow at the point where they emerge from the ground and they expand upward in an inverted taper, so that their effect on the eye is a sense of weight and force poised in the air, beyond the world. Thought by some to be a part of an otherwise vanished circle, the standing stones of Kilchattan have also been described as possible remnants of a Druid astronomical observatory. Donald Gibbie told me that the crofter on whose croft they stand once tried to start a post-hole by jamming a four-foot crowbar into the ground between the two stones, and the crowbar disappeared into the earth – into some kind of subterranean chamber – and has never been recovered. The stones, tall and slim, are visible from a long distance up the glen of Kilchattan. They are dark against the sky, and they stand in a field of grain. They are called Fingal's Limpet Hammers.

A piper once entered a cave on the northern shore of Kilchattan playing 'The Lament for Donald Ban Mac-Crimmon'. He was followed by his dog. The piper was never seen again, but the dog eventually reappeared five miles away, on the coast of Balaromin Mor, and the dog's hair was scorched. So goes the legend of the Piper's Cave. Colonsay had its outsize beings as well as its little people. They were known as the Fomorian Giants, and their mother, the Cailleach, was the spirit of winter. She had a single eye, just above her nose. She kept a young girl captive, and eventually the girl's lover attacked the Cailleach, who avoided his assaults by turning herself into a grey headland, always moist, above the sea. This is Cailleach Uragaig, where Donald Gibbie stood on the pinnacle rock of the McNeill lairds. It was said for centuries that *maighdean mhara* (mermaids) sat among the skerries combing their hair at night. The ichthyic sheaths that covered their lower parts were removable. An islander could keep a mermaid as long as he kept her fishskin, but when she recovered it she would always put it on again and vanish into the sea. The largest creature anyone had ever heard of was the Great Beast of the Ocean, and to give an idea of its size people said that seven herring are a salmon's fill, seven salmon are a seal's fill, seven seals are a whale's fill, and seven whales are the fill of the Great Beast of the Ocean. The smallest creature anyone had ever heard of was the gigelorum, which made its nest in the mite's ear, and this is all that was known about it. If a cuckoo cried from the roof of a house, a death would come to that house that year. If your nose itched, you knew that a letter would soon be delivered to you. If your mouth itched, a dram was coming. If your ears tingled, a friend had died and the news would come soon. If your elbow itched, you knew that you would soon sleep with a stranger. Turning a boat around, passing out drams, walking around a house you were about to enter – you went to the right. You did all such things in the direction that corresponded to the course of the sun. When a young woman combed her hair at night, she put every loose strand in the fire. If the hair did not burn, it meant she would one day drown.

If a girl did drown, she might become a seal. Then once a year she could, if she liked, step out of her phocine skin and walk the earth as a human being. The shores of the Hebrides have always been populated with seal maidens, sunning themselves on boulders above the waves, their sealskins draped nearby. Once, a mainland girl betrothed to a young man of Colonsay was drowned on the voyage she was making to the island to marry him. In his melancholy, he hunted the shores for years, and finally he found her. He stole her sealskin and hid it, and then he took her home with him. He married her. Seal maidens could live among mortals and could marry and have children, and frequently enough they did, but they always felt a powerful draw to the sea, which they sometimes found irresistible. This one bore the children of the man of Colonsay and had good years with him, but her longing for the ocean finally overcame her. She found the sealskin where her husband had hidden it, and she disappeared. This is the germinal story of the original clan of Colonsay. From her children – so the legend goes – the clan proliferated.

From their earliest beginnings in the eleventh century, to their full development, in the thirteenth century, to the Battle of Culloden, April 16, 1746, the clans lasted seven hundred years. In the nineteenth century, during the Pan-European wave of Highland nostalgia when Angus MacKay was piping for Queen Victoria and Felix Mendelssohn was writing the 'Scotch Symphony' and his concert overture 'The Hebrides', the Scottish artist R. R. McIan completed a memorial set of watercolour portraits of Highland clan chiefs, and these portraits have ever since been regarded as the best of their kind. McIan's chief of Colonsay appears on the shore of the island, the hills of Jura rising in the distance over the water behind him, and the look in his eyes, as he stares – full of attention – out to sea, suggests that whatever boredom his island life may cause him is frequently relieved. He appears to be relatively young still, but only moderately fit. Beneath his long shirt of chain mail there is an obvious paunch. He is dressed for feud. His left hand is on his hip. His right hand holds two spears. Hanging from a rent in the chain mail is a sword that must weigh twenty-five pounds. His boots are of un-tanned leather. He wears a conical helmet of the type the Vikings used, and it is decorated with an upthrust-ing eagle's wing. His beard is full and has an auburn glint. When he was first acknowledged as chief, he stood on top of a cairn, holding in his hand a white rod that symbolized his responsibilities, and he swore that he would preserve the customs of the people, one of which was that without regard to one's position in the clan it was every clansman's first duty to go to the aid of any other clansman in time of need. A bard then recited several hundred verses in his praise. He became chief because he was, at the time, considered the fittest mem-ber of his family, and thus did not necessarily succeed his father nor will he necessarily be succeeded by his own son. The tanist, heir apparent to the chief's posi-tion, may be a brother, a cousin, a nephew, and the tanist's power is considerable – he is the administrative trustee of the lands of the clan. When the chief replaces his chain mail, he will put on his plaid – a huge bolt of tartan cloth, two yards wide, about six yards long. He drapes it around himself in careful pleats – the arche-typal kilt – and holds it in place with a leather belt and a brooch at the shoulder. When he travels, he sleeps in his plaid and nothing more, even in snow. The tartan cloth is dyed with vegetable extracts that yield colours so soft that the tartan all but blends into a background of heather. The women of the clan wear tartan shawls, and flowing tartan or plain-coloured gowns that are secured with brooches. Over their hair, they wear linen that is fastened beneath their chins. The clansmen eat barley cakes and oatcakes for breakfast and barley cakes and oatcakes for lunch. The meats for dinner – mutton, venison, beef – are boiled in the stomach of the animal they came from. The preparation of meals is simpler during hunting or feuding expeditions. The flesh of killed animals is squeezed to reduce the blood content, and then eaten. The clansmen eat fish, too, and in token of the sense of equality that pervades the clan, everyone's fishing line is by custom the same length. The chief has lighted his share of fires at the mouths of caves on other islands in order to choke to death the hiding families of his enemies, and with his heavy sword he has performed decapitations, sometimes retaining as trophies the heads he has severed. In times of major purpose, he has fought beside the very people who might otherwise have been killing him or he them. With them all, as Scott would one day remember, he answered the summons to Bannockburn.

> Lochbuie's fierce and warlike lord
> Their signal saw, and grasped his sword,
> And verdant Islay called her host,
> And the clans of Jura's rugged coast
>   Lord Ronald's call obey,
> And Scarba's isle, whose tortured shore
> Still rings to Corrievrekan's roar,
>   And lonely Colonsay.

The stream was not entirely red. The clan's name implied that its people were people of peace, and the chief made some effort to alleviate the irony. The parliaments of the isles were held on a small island in Loch Finlagan, on Islay, and at these councils – attended by the clan chiefs of the Hebrides and presided over by the Lord of the Isles – the chief from Colonsay kept a journal of what went on. He was the traditional secretary, recorder, scribe. After the clan was broken, all records kept by the chiefs of Colonsay was destroyed by the MacDonalds, so what was written is unknown, but one hopes that beyond the drone of deliberations certain details were not omitted – the passing of the goblet full of true cognac, imported by twenty-oared galley from France; the exertions of the Orator, a bardlike functionary who composed his speeches by lying on his back with a huge rock on his stomach, the idea being that golden rhetoric would thereby more thoroughly be pressed out through his brain. The chief also was present, among the chiefs of the larger clans, at a colloquium held on the island of Iona, where he and the others wrote and signed the Statutes of Icolmekill. In this document, the men of the isles reluctantly acknowledged the course of history as it was developing and decreed that certain children of the clans should be sent to Lowland schools to learn English.

On a shoulder of the hill of the Candle Cairn, in Scalasaig, the chief of Colonsay built a fort called Dunevin. Its ruins are still there, beneath sod, and are most evident from a distance, for the top of the rise is square, with green ramparts. The islanders call it the Green Hill. Heather apparently won't grow where the earth has been disturbed by the battlements of the past. The view from Dunevin, once protective, is now merely spectacular, with the other hills and ranges of Colonsay paying out in all directions above the island's glens, surrounded by the framing sea. In the fields below Dunevin, the clansmen once harvested with scythes.

They threshed with flails. The grain was eventually ground in hand querns. While all this was going on, the chief, it seems likely, was sitting around petting his black dog, perhaps at Dunevin, perhaps at his house in Kiloran. The black dog was a matter of some discussion on the island, because no one could understand why the chief wanted to keep it. The dog was lazy, would not hunt, and ate prodigious amounts of food. 'Kill it,' said the clansmen, but the chief said no, the day would come when he would be glad he had the dog.

From these beginnings emerged one of the most widely known legends of the Hebrides. It was said that the chief had been hunting in a remote part of the island when he came to a cottage inhabited by an old man who had a litter of pups, one of which, a black one, was so appealing to the chief that he said, 'This dog will be my own.'

The old man said, 'You may have your choice of the other pups, but you will not get that one.'

'I will not take any but this one,' said the chief.

'Since you are resolved to have it, you may have it,' said the old man. 'It will not do you but one day's service, but it will do that well.'

The dog grew to be large, powerful, beautiful, hungry, and – because it refused to hunt – worthless. Once, the chief arranged to go hunting on Jura, and he tried to take the dog, but the dog looked at the shore and the waiting boat and lay down and refused to move.

'Kill it,' said the rest of the hunting party.

The chief said, 'No. The black dog's day has not come yet.'

A forbidding wind came up and the hunt was postponed. The next day, the boat was prepared again, but the dog would not go.

'Kill it and don't be feeding it any longer,' said the clansmen.

'I will not kill it,' said the chief. 'The black dog's day will come yet.'

The sky became violent and the expedition was postponed.

'The dog has foreknowledge,' said the clansmen.

'It has foreknowledge that its own day will come yet,' said the chief.

The next day, in clear and lovely weather, the hunting party, seventeen in all, got into the boat – everyone, the chief included, ignoring the black dog. Just as they were about to shove off, the dog ran down to the shore and leaped into the boat. 'The black dog's day is drawing near,' said the chief.

That night, in a cave on Jura, the chief's sixteen companions were murdered by supernatural beings who tried to attack the chief, too, but were driven away by the ferocious black dog. Then the life of the chief was almost taken by a great arm and hand that reached down for him through a cleft in the ceiling of the cave. The black dog soared into the air and locked its jaws over the forearm of this monster and chewed it until the hand fell to the floor of the cave. The black dog went out and chased the bloodied monster away, then returned to the feet of the chief, lay down, and died. '*Thig latha choindui fhathast*' is a Gaelic expression that derives from this legend and is in common use. It says, literally, 'The black dog's day will come yet,' but in English it has been slightly corrupted into 'Every dog will have his day'.

For putting that one over, I cannot help but feel affection for the chief, and it even makes forgivable, perhaps, his slipping the sword and the galley onto his tombstone and absurdly pretending to be a Lord of the Isles. I have on my living-room wall in Princeton a six-foot rubbing of his tombstone, elaborate with ivy, harts, and griffins; it is there because it always makes me smile. The chief in that particular incarnation was the one who died in the cave in Uragaig when the MacLean bowman shot him from above. An hour or so beforehand, he had been at his house, in Kiloran, when the invading MacLeans approached. Outnumbered, he left in a hurry with one of his friends, whose name was Gilbert MacMillan. They were running together up the side of Ben Sgoltaire when they looked behind them into the glen and saw thirty or forty MacLeans go into the house and come back out dragging McPhee's screaming wife.

McPhee said, 'MacMillan, why don't you go down and see if you can do something to help her? She has been good to you, MacMillan. She gave you the stockings you wear. And you gave her good promises that you would see no harm come to her.'

'Unlucky is the time that you remind me of it,' Mac-Millan said, and he drew his sword and went back down the hill. MacLeans swarmed around him, but he stood with his back to a high stone wall and magnificently began to hack them down. Swinging and thrusting, he killed sixteen MacLeans, and he might have killed them all, but other MacLeans went around to the other side of the wall and pushed out stones at the base, making a hole through which they chopped at MacMillan's legs until he fell. McPhee went on up the hill. One associates with one's ancestors at one's risk. I will never again be able to look a MacMillan in the eye.

Josie's Well

The Laphroaig distillery is on the southern shore of Islay, one of the isles of Argyll, in the Inner Hebrides. The buildings are all white and rise among dark-green Scotch pines by the water's edge. A clear burn flows to the distillery through acres of peats, over rocks, more peats, more rocks, more peats, into the buildings and out in barrels and bottles of the whisky, Laphroaig. The distiller's home is a part of the compound and is full of light, for its seaward walls are largely glass. His living room is upstairs and is cantilevered toward a spectacular and often misty view over the pines and the sea. Multiple white couches are covered with pillows in blazing colour. The bar is quilted. There is a white grand piano. Two golden retrievers lie on the floor. The distiller, whose name is Wishart Campbell, stands beside a Sony solid-state stereo tape recorder, his hand on the bass control. He wears a sport jacket, and he is somewhat heavyset but nonetheless athletic in carriage, a glib man, quick, fluid, idiomatic. He refers to his wife as 'Mrs C'. His whisky is so smoky, so heavy, so redolently peaty that a consumer feels he is somehow drinking a slab of bacon. There is some Laphroaig – a few drops per fifth – in Ballantine's, Teacher's, Dewar's, White Horse, Johnnie Walker, Black & White, Haig & Haig, thirty-odd Scotches in all. 'If the blenders want a Hebridean malt, they come here and get it,' Campbell explains. 'In a proper blend, Laphroaig is the foundation, the real gutsy base.' George Gershwin's 'Love Walked In' is pouring out of the Sony. Campbell turns the bass control knob as far as it will go, and the Gershwin deepens into broad profundities of sound. Campbell says, 'There you have it. That is the Laphroaig.'

The Talisker distillery is also by the sea, by a long, narrow bay on the western coast of the Isle of Skye. Talisker was a farmer who grew barley. In 1834, he began to roast it over burning peat, ferment it with yeast and water, distil the resulting wash, and then sell – 'A wee drop of himself', as Skye men say – the whisky that continues to carry his name. A syndicate with headquarters in London owns Talisker's distillery now, and the syndicate has installed as general manager Peter Hogg, a young and serious man with tie and pullover, bright eyes, dark hair, a dangling forelock. Hogg grew up in whisky in the way that some people are born to the stage. He belongs to Craigellachie, a Speyside town, seat of the great Macallan distillery. He is knowledgeable, modern, and technical. He explains that barley is the choice of grains because barley seeds have a high content of starch and, further, are protected by double skins, so air has less chance to get at the starch and produce mold. He explains that germination of the seeds promotes the enzyme diastase which, in hot water, helps convert the starch to the sugar that will ferment into alcohol.

Hogg opens a door at one end of a germinating floor (where barley is four inches deep and doves fly through open windows to help themselves) and he steps into the kiln. The floor of the kiln, a gridwork of thousands of thin metallic plates, is covered with several inches of germinated barley, and the smoke of peat that is burning below filters up through the grid. When the barley goes into the kiln it is known as green malt. Distillers use coke as well as peat for their fires, and the ratio they choose determines the peatiness of the ultimate whisky. Unblended, pure Highland malt whiskies are made in only a few places in Scotland – in the Hebrides, on the Mull of Kintyre, and in the riparian counties of the River Spey. They vary in taste as pronouncedly as regional wines. Talisker, on the tongue, unique among the malts, is halfway between the characteristically heavy flavours of the island whiskies and the patrician subtleties of Speyside.

By an entirely different and much cheaper process, whisky is also made in Scotland from corn. It is called grain whisky, as distinguished from malt whisky, and it is very nearly tasteless. A bottle of blended Scotch whisky consists mainly of grain whisky and is flavoured by various malts. The malts are known as the top-dressing, and the grain whisky is known as the pad. In some blended whiskies there are as many as forty different malts, sitting on the pad. Twenty is average. Blended whisky, bland and facile, was developed for bland Americans, who drink most of the whisky distilled in Scotland. Highlanders, who can't tell the difference between one blend and another, roll on the floor in laughter at the thought of American sophisticates who think they can. Meanwhile, they drink their ranging malts, resonant as cognac, and so replete with flavour that a few drops are enough to perform an aromatic alchemy.

The barley has roasted for forty-eight hours and is now, in the term of the trade, malted. Peter Hogg picks up some of the seeds and eats them, like malted peanuts. They are delicious. It is dram time. Twice daily, the men working in the distillery – malt men, mill men, wash men, tun-room men, still men, some twenty-five in all – line up for their dram. At Talisker, the whisky comes in a copper jug from the warehouse, and is poured into

something called 'the horn'. It is a two-inch segment of
cattle horn, fitted with a metallic bottom. Carved on it
are the words *A Wee Doch an Doris*, 'a wee drink before
you leave'. Everybody drinks a full measure from the
horn – everybody but Peter Hogg and the government
excise man. Each distillery has its resident excise man.
This one is a Londoner, outposted far up here on Skye,
a decent enough chap. 'He turns a blind eye to the
horn,' says Peter Hogg. 'For myself, I taste the whisky
but I never drink it. It would take a very special occasion
to get me to drink it. Working with it, it's not policy to
drink it. One might get addicted to it. I smell it once a
week to see if there's enough peat in it. When I drink
something, I like a little beer.'

Wishart Campbell, of Laphroaig, generously and almost
evangelistically presses Laphroaig on friends and strangers alike. But after booming up his hi-fi, he moves to
the quilted bar to fix his own drink, Demerara rum and
Pepsi-Cola.

It is a beautiful afternoon in Banffshire. The lush,
green, rural valley of the Spey is ablaze with mustard-
coloured whin. The river is fast and occasionally shivers
with white water. The sky is clear. The air is warm. The
branches of birches and pines move in a moderate wind.
Distillers hate a day like this. It's bad for germination,
bad for whisky. Too many days like this could put a
distillery out of business. Whisky thrives on gloom, fog,
rain. Above the Spey in Macallan Parish, Craigellachie,
is the Macallan Distillery, which collects water from the
Ringorm Burn and from various springs in the local
gneiss and produces one of the three malt whiskies that
are by general consent regarded as the best distilled in
Scotland. The other two distilleries – J. & J. Grant, and
George and J. G. Smith – are only a few miles away.

The executive offices in the Macallan Distillery are expensively designed, darkly panelled, shining with polished wooden desk and table surfaces and rich leather upholstery, and could be the offices of a remarkably successful law firm in London. The offices have emptied out at the end of the working day. George Harbinson, managing director and chairman, is there alone. He is a slim man, bald. At the back of his head is a thick fringe of curly silver hair. His manner is quiet. His face is sensitive and in its strong lines there is a suggestion, among other things, of melancholy, but he seems to be only mildly put out by the lovely weather. He wears a dark suit and holds in his hand a narrow, stemmed glass that is tapered toward the top and partly filled with Macallan Pure Highland Malt Scotch Whisky. He adds a little water 'to bring out the nose'. He inhales the aroma. He seems to like what he is doing. 'When it's free, it has a very sweet, aromatic nose to it,' Harbinson says. 'It makes me immediately think of mountain air.'

The whisky in his glass was made in 1950, drawn from the cask in 1962, and is part of Macallan's 'library', or, perhaps more appropriately, *bibliothèque*, kept for the record, to assure the continuity of standard.

'Other single whiskies have a heavier nose,' he goes on. 'We don't aim to have a heavily peated malt.' He sips. 'One has to drink in moderation,' he says. 'Otherwise one wouldn't last very long. Many years ago, they used to say that whisky was old if it was cool from the stills. It went straight to the pubs. The body gets along better with older whisky. In maturer whisky, you've got rid of a lot of the lighter, rather objectionable alcohols.'

Twelve years is the prime age, most agree, but Harbinson dissents. He thinks whisky gets better the longer it ages. Whisky is sold the day it is made, but is stored by the maker. In the vastness of the warehouses, barrels sometimes become misplaced and are found many years after they would otherwise have been delivered. Such a barrel was recently found at Macallan. The whisky in it was thirty-five years old, and Harbinson places it among the best he has ever tasted.

The greatness of Macallan whisky, Harbinson says, is 'a matter of luck – the people that developed the plant happened onto the right shape of stills.' Barley soup ferments in tuns and is then boiled away in wash stills. The resulting liquor – called low wine – is boiled again in spirit stills. The wash stills are tall and bulbous, often shaped like lamp glasses; the spirit stills are smaller and conical, suggesting the hats of leprechauns. All are copper, for the heat transfer is better in copper than in any other metal. Much in the way that Ph.D. candidates will fasten upon and attempt to explicate a great work of the imagination, minor and would-be distillers examine the stills of a place like Macallan. Some distilleries permit no photographs, nervously keeping to themselves the exact curve of the shoulders, the style of the ogee, the relative grace of the swan neck, the size and attitude of the lynne arm. The lynne arm extends away from the uppermost part of the still, above the neck, and carries the vaporous liquor to the condenser. Some lynne arms curve like the tops of coat hangers. Others wiggle away in right angles. Some are narrow, some wide. The lynne arms at Talisker go straight out horizontally, as if to suggest that there will be no nonsense at Talisker. The lynne arms at Macallan are extraordinarily thick – about fourteen inches in diameter – and slope downward on a gentle grade. Harbinson seems to doubt that this could open the secret of Macallan.

'The way a plant is operated is as important as the design,' he says. 'You get better whisky if you run fairly slowly. Modern demand causes many distilleries to run fast. We have small, individual stills. Like anything else you are cooking, smaller boilings are better for flavour.'

When the whisky runs out of the condensers it is as clear and colourless as water. Whether it is heavy or light it all looks like water, and the amount of colour that is ultimately given to it is almost strictly a matter of show business. Whisky is aged in casks of new oak, or in used casks that previously held sherry. The sherry colours the whisky. If the maker wants a light-coloured whisky, he uses fewer sherry casks per lot. Makers try to match the colour to what they think the taste is, but colour of whisky has nothing whatever to do with its true lightness. Harbinson is holding his glass up before a window in what is now fading daylight. 'Sherry does, to a minor extent, affect the taste of the spirit,' he says in a ruminative way. 'We've tried putting it in refilled whisky casks, in brandy casks, in Madeira casks, but the whisky was a wee bit spiritous. Freshly emptied sherry casks are the best. They placate the spirit. They calm it down.'

Macallan and J. & J. Grant's Glen Grant together form the baseline of the triumvirate of malt whisky. The apex above them is George & J. G. Smith's The Glenlivet, the finest whisky made in Scotland. Why do the Scots think so? What is the secret of The Glenlivet? Could it be the altitude? The distillery is the highest in Scotland, but is only nine hundred feet above sea level. Is it the Livet? The Livet is a clear, tumbling tributary of the Spey, but the distillery uses its water only as a coolant. Is it the shape of the stills? the quality of the malt? the source of the peats? Or is the nature of the whisky in the nature of the man, the owner, the chairman, who now, in his offices in the distillery, waves a brace of pistols that his great-grandfather, the founder, was the last man to fire in anger? The two greatest individual names in the history of malt whisky are Smith and Grant, and this man's name is Captain Smith Grant.

He went to Downside and Sandhurst, years ago. There could be little doubt that he would have retired from the army as Field Marshal Smith Grant had he not gone back to the stills in his youth. He is in his sixties, tall, powerfully framed, with a large head, a heavy face, and a look that, despite its elements of weariness, suggests that life has been good in Glenlivet. Captain Smith Grant seems completely unbound, and in that sense must be the loosest man in the Highlands. He wears his Highland Brigade tie and his kilt in Hunting Grant. He waves his great-grandfather's pistols. 'Venomous-looking things, are they not?' he says. 'I mean, if you got hit with a bullet out of *that* . . .' His full-bodied voice fades for a moment as he thinks about his whisky and the process by which it is made. 'There's nothing secret about any of it,' he says. 'It just happens that it comes out like that. People come here and ask if they can measure the stills. "Measure them," I say. "Photograph them. Do anything you like with them so long as you leave them here." Many people have copied them. Actually, we chucked out a still three years ago that was ninety-eight years old. We put in a new one and it didn't seem to affect anything. We buy our peats from a subcontractor in Tomintoul. We're using British barley, the same barley everyone else uses. We *have* used California barley, Danubian barley, Karachi barley – Tunisian, Australian, Danish island barley. It isn't the barley. We can't be bothered malting our own barley. We buy it from maltsters in the south of Scotland.'

Captain Smith Grant takes a walk around his distillery. It is a beautifully unprepossessing compound of buildings set in high, open, hill country, looking out over a field of oats in which stand the semi-ruins of Blairfindy Castle. The distillery – its long, low buildings covered with roughcast; its eaves, window frames, and doorways painted dark red – might be a dairy farm. Its warehouses, full of butts and hogsheads stacked over an earth floor (some think the best whisky ages closest to the dank ground), reek of malt whisky. The Glenlivet wash stills, plump and very narrow-waisted, are buxom. There are just two of them, twenty-five feet high, pure copper, and they look remarkably like a pair of tightly bodiced Victorian women, hardly promising as vessels for the gestation of a drink whose very name in Gaelic – *uisge-beatha* – means 'the water of life'. The lynne arms droop unimaginatively. The spirit stills, also two in number, are small replicas of the wash stills.

'It's not really the stills,' says Captain Smith Grant. 'I think it's ninety-nine and a half per cent the water – the water, and a sort of certain fiddle-faddle in the manufacture. The water comes from Josie's Well. Who Josie was I don't know, but the water comes from Josie's Well.'

Talking all the way, Captain Smith Grant goes out the front door of his distillery, crosses the road, lifts his kilt, climbs a fence and moves through the waist-deep golden oats toward Josie's Well. He regards the hike as insanity – 'to see a bloody hole in the ground' – but he is cheerfully willing to go. 'The Invergordon people thought they would expand into the malt market a few years ago, and they built a distillery just up the road here, built a distillery to produce a million gallons a year,' he says. 'They're struggling to get about two hundred thousand gallons. They make bloody awful whisky. We think it rather heavy. They're not in the same watershed, quite. We produce seven hundred and fifty thousand gallons a year. Ninety-eight per cent of it goes into blended whiskies. John Walker uses thirty thousand gallons of The Glenlivet a year, Black or Red, we don't know. We fill large orders from Haig, and so forth. Our job is to sell to the blenders. They use The Glenlivet as a top-dressing, to cover up the multitude of sins in the vat, to give it some sort of quality. People have spread the fact that there is nothing to touch The Glenlivet, so we must eternally turn out the same whisky. We could make it more cheaply, but we don't dare try. It might change it. It is a full-bodied, slow-maturing whisky which has a great deal of quality. The Scotch whisky trade have come to rely on it as an unaltering standard.'

This reminds him of the way the name of his whisky has been poached and poached again, and he fulminates. His is the one distillery in Glenlivet, but whisky-makers all over Strathspey have long made use of the name, slipping the word Glenlivet onto their labels in order to arrogate to themselves some of The Glenlivet's stature.

'In the United Kingdom, you can't have a geographical name as a trademark,' he explains. 'That's why they've had so much trouble over Harris tweed. A few years ago, damned near all whisky was labelled as coming from Glenlivet. Glenlivet was the longest glen in Scotland, with all the people stealing the name.' He pronounces the name *glen leave it*, although nearly everyone else in Scotland says *glen live it*. 'We've succeeded in shoving everybody off,' he continues. 'We took the case up to the House of Lords and spent God knows what, about twenty thousand quid. The people of Speyside argued that they put Livet water in their whisky, for the Livet flows into the Spey. We should have put the Provost of Grant into the box and asked him where he puts Grantown sewage. He would have had to say that that, too, goes into the Spey. All whisky distilleries use water from springs and burns, anyway, not from rivers. Rivers are too dangerous. The water is different at different times. We settled it, finally, after a fashion. These people in Speyside have to hyphenate the name Glenlivet with their own name, if they're going to use Glenlivet. And they have to print both names the same size – Glenfarclas-Glenlivet, Mortlach-Glenlivet, Longmorn-Glenlivet, Linkwood-Glenlivet, nearly all of them do it. The full name of the Macallan company is R. Kemp,

Macallan-Glenlivet. But our whisky is The Glenlivet, and no one else can call their whisky simply that.'

Striding on, he drops into a calmer mood. 'Macallan is nice whisky. I had some two years ago. Glenfarclas is a very nice little whisky, but it has no particular stature or character. It's a well-made, above-average Highland malt. I had some seven years ago. Glen Grant is a thinner whisky than The Glenlivet. It does not have the same body. It's sweet, and useful for blending. I had some last fall. A drop or two of water brings out the nose. I know no one who does not drink whisky with water. There doesn't seem to be much future in just knocking it back. You have half a taste of it and it's gone.'

In the middle of the oat field is a small, fenced enclosure, eight feet square. The fence is made of wood so old that it is dark grey and covered with lichen. Three rails are broken down. Bits of rusted wire hold the rest together. Sheep that have somehow got into the field have left wool on the barbs of the wire. On the ground, among weeds and buttercups in the middle of the enclosure, is a large flagstone five inches thick. Grant heaves away the slab. Beneath it is – just as he said – a mere hole in the ground, almost square at the surface, eighteen inches across, and fully five feet deep. At the bottom, water voluminously rushes out of the earth, out of some fateful crack in the granite of the glen, whirling, eddying, prodigiously, noisily gurgling. A three-inch pipe carries it under the oats to the distillery.

'What if Josie's Well should ever go dry?'

'It's not allowed to go dry. We couldn't do without it.'

Grant's kilt is blowing in the wind. He leans on the fence. A rail cracks. He almost falls.

'Why don't you build a brick enclosure here? Why don't you make a shrine out of this place?'

'If someone mucks about with that well, it may

disappear. The mason may put his foot in it. I think we can class ourselves as fairly prosperous. We want to stay that way.'

Captain Smith Grant is hungry from the open air, and after returning from the oat field has his lunch. Beforehand, he pours a glass of The Glenlivet, drops just enough water into it for a perfect nose, and hands it to me. Then he mixes for himself a gin and tonic.

On the edge of Invermoriston Forest, I was trying to explain raised beaches, the fifty-foot beaches of Scotland, so called because they are about that far above the sea. Waves never touch them. Tides don't come near reaching them. Shell and shingle, whitened like bones, they are after-effects of the ice, two miles thick, that once rested on Scotland and actually shoved Scotland down into the earth. When the ice melted, the sea slowly came up, but so did the land, sluggishly recovering its buoyancy over the molten centre of things. After the sea had increased as much as it was going to, the land kept rising, and beaches were lifted into the air, some as much as fifty feet.

That was how I understood the story, and I was doing what I could to say it in a way that would make it intelligible to an audience of four children (mine – all girls, and all quite young), but the distractions were so numerous that I never really had a chance. My family and I were having a lakeside lunch – milk, potato sticks, lambs' tongues, shortbread, white chocolate, Mini-Dunlop cheese – beside a stream in a grove of birches that was backed by dense reforested pines. The pines covered steep slopes toward summits two thousand feet above us. It was late spring, but there were snowfields up there nonetheless, and the water we drank had been snow in the mountains that morning

Near us, another family, also with small children, was

having what was evidently a birthday picnic. They had arrived after we were already settled, and they had chosen – I don't know why, with acre upon acre of unpeopled and essentially similar terrain to move about in – to unpack all their special effects (a glistening white cake, noisemakers, conical cardboard orange hats) only forty or fifty yards away. I tried to ignore them and go on with my ruminations on the raised beaches. There were no raised beaches in that place, at least not in the usual form, but the children had seen them and had played on them elsewhere in the Highlands, and I thought that if they could understand how such pheno-mena had come to be, they might in turn be able to imagine the great, long lake now before them – Loch Ness – as the sea loch, the arm of the Atlantic, that it once was, and how marine creatures in exceptional variety had once freely moved in and out of it, some inevitably remaining.

Losing interest in the birthday party, my youngest daughter said, 'I want to see the monster.'

This had already become another distraction. In much the way that, in the United States, 'No Hunting' signs are posted on every other tree along blacktop country roads, cardboard signs of about the same size had been tacked to trees and poles along the lake. There were several in the birch grove. Printed in royal blue on a white background, they said, 'Any members of the general public who genuinely believe they have seen an unusual creature or object in or on the shores of Loch Ness are requested to report the occurrence to Expedi-tion Headquarters at Achnahannet, two miles south of Urquhart Castle. If unable to report in person, they may telephone the Expedition (No. Drumnadrochit 358). Reports will only be of interest from people willing to give their full name and address and fill in a Sighting Report Form, which will be sent on request. Thank you for your co-operation. Published by the Loch Ness Phenomena Investigation Bureau, 23 Ashley Place, London, SW1, and printed at the Courier Office, Inverness.'

'What makes you think the monster wants to see *you*?' I said to my youngest one. 'There won't be any sightings today, anyway. There's too much wind out there.'

The wind on the lake was quite strong. It was blowing from the north. There were whitecaps, and the ranks of the waves were uniform in our perspective, which was high. Watching the waves, I remembered canoe trips when I was ten or eleven years old, trying to achieve some sort of momentum against white-capping head-winds between Rogers Rock and Sabbath Day Point on Lake George. Lake George was for beginners, who could learn in its unwild basin the essentials they would need to know on longer trips in later years in wilder-nesses they would seek out. But now, watching the north wind go down the lake in Scotland, I could not remem-ber headwinds anywhere as powerful and savage as they had been in that so-styled lake for beginners, and I could feel again the skin rubbed off my hands. The likeness was in more than the wind, however. It was in the appearance, the shape, and the scale – about a mile from side to side – of Loch Ness, which, like the Ameri-can lake, is at least twenty times longer than it is wide, a long deep cleft, positioned like some great geophysical axe-cut between its lateral hills. I remember being told, around the fire at night, stories of the first white man who saw Lake George. He was a travelling French priest, intent on converting the Mohawks and other nations of the Iroquois. He had come from Orléans. He said that the lake was the most beautiful he had ever seen, and he named it the Lake of the Blessed Sacrament. The Indians, observing that the priest blessed them with his right hand, held him down and chewed away his fingers until the fingers were stumps and the hand was pulp. Later, when the priest did not stop his work, the Indians axed the top of his skull and then cut off his head.

Lake George is so clear that objects far below its surface, such as white stones or hovering bass, can be seen in total definition. The water of Loch Ness is so dark with the tints of peat that on a flat-calm day it looks like black glass. Three or four feet below the surface is an obscurity so complete that experienced divers have retreated from it in frustration, and in some cases in fear. A swimmer looking up toward a bright sky from a distance of inches beneath the surface has the impression that he is afloat in very dark tea. Lake George is nearly two hundred feet deep in places, has numerous islands, and with its bays and points is prototypal of beautiful mountain lakes of grand dimension in every part of the world. Loch Ness is like almost no other lake anywhere. Its shores are formidably and somewhat unnaturally parallel. It has no islands. Its riparian walls go straight down. Its bottom is flat, and in most places is seven hundred feet deep, a mean depth far greater than the mean depth of the North Sea. Loch Ness holds a fantastic volume of water, the entire runoff of any number of northern glens – Glen Affric, Glen Cannich, Glen Moriston, Glen Farrar, Glen Urquhart. All of these valleys, impressive in themselves, are petals to Glen More, the Great Glen. Loch Ness is the principal basin of the Great Glen, and the Great Glen is the epicentre of the Highlands. A few miles of silt, carried into the lake by the rivers, long ago dammed the seaward end, changing the original sea loch into a freshwater lake, but so slowly that marine creatures trapped within it had a chance to adapt themselves. Meanwhile the land kept rising, and with it the new lake. The surface of Loch Ness is fifty-two feet above sea level.

My wife listened with some interest when, repeating

all this, I made an expanded attempt to enrich everyone's experience, but nothing was going through to the children. 'I want to see the monster,' the youngest one said again, speaking for all. They didn't want to know how or why the so-called monster might have come into that particular lake. They just wanted to see it. But the wind was not slowing up out there on the lake.

All of us looked now at the family that was having the birthday picnic, for the father had stood up shouting and had flung a large piece of the birthday cake at his wife. It missed her and spattered in bits in the branches of a tree. She shouted back at him something to the effect that he was depraved and cruel, and he in turn bellowed that she was a carbon of her bloody mother and that he was fed up. She said she had had all she could ever take, and was going home – to England, apparently. With that, she ran up the hillside and soon was out of sight in the pines. At first, he did not follow, but he suddenly was on his feet and shouting serial threats as he too went out of range in the pines. Meanwhile, their children, all but one, were crying. The one that wasn't crying was the girl whose birthday it was, and she just sat without moving, under a conical orange hat, staring emptily in the direction of the lake.

We went to our car and sat in it for some time, trying not to be keeping too obvious an eye on the children in the birch grove, who eventually began to play at being the bailiffs of the birthday picnic and made such a mess that finally the girl whose birthday it was began to cry, and she was still crying when her father came out of the pines. I then drove north.

The road – the A-82 – stayed close to the lake, often on ledges that had been blasted into the mountainsides. The steep forests continued, broken now and again, on one shore or the other, by fields of fern, clumps of bright-yellow whin, and isolated stands of cedar. Along the far shore were widely separated houses and farms, which to the eyes of a traveller appeared almost unbelievably luxuriant after the spare desolation of some of the higher glens. We came to the top of the rise and suddenly saw, on the right-hand side of the road, on the edge of a high meadow that sloped sharply a considerable distance to the lake, a cluster of caravans and other vehicles, arranged in the shape of a C, with an opening toward the road – much like a circle of prairie schooners formed for protection against savage attack. All but one or two of the vehicles were painted bright lily-pad green. The compound, in its compact half acre, was surrounded by a fence, to keep out, among other things, sheep which were grazing all over the slope in deep-green turf among buttercups, daisies, and thistles. Gulls above beat hard into the wind, then turned and planed toward the south. Gulls are inland birds in Scotland, there being so little distance from anywhere to the sea. A big fireplace had been made from rocks of the sort that were scattered all over the meadow. And on the lakeward side a platform had been built, its level eminence emphasizing the declivity of the hill, which dropped away below it. Mounted on the platform was a thirty-five millimetre motion-picture camera with an enormous telephoto lens. From its point of view, two hundred feet above the lake and protruding like a gargoyle, the camera could take in a bedazzling panorama that covered thousands of acres of water.

This was Expedition Headquarters, the principal field station of the Loch Ness Phenomena Investigation Bureau – dues five pounds per annum, life membership one hundred pounds, tax on donations recoverable under covenant. Those who join the bureau receive newsletters and annual reports, and are eligible to participate in the fieldwork if they so desire. I turned into the compound and parked between two bright green reconditioned old London taxis. The central area had long since been worn grassless, and was covered at this moment with fine-grain dust. People were coming and going. The place seemed rather public, as if it were a depot. No one even halfway interested in the natural history of the Great Glen would think of driving up the A-82 without stopping in there. Since the A-82 is the principal route between Glasgow and Inverness, it is not surprising that the apparently amphibious creature as yet unnamed, the so-called Loch Ness Monster, has been seen not only from the highway but on it.

The atmosphere around the headquarters suggested a scientific frontier and also a boom town, much as Cape Canaveral and Cocoa Beach do. There were, as well, cirrus wisps of show business and fine arts. Probably the one word that might have been applied to everyone present was adventurer. There was, at any rate, nothing emphatically laboratorial about the place, although the prevailing mood seemed to be one not of holiday but of matter-of-fact application and patient dedication. A telephone call came in that day, to the caravan that served as an office, from a woman who owned an inn south of Inverarigaig, on the other side of the lake. She said that she had seen the creature that morning just forty yards offshore – three humps, nothing else to report, and being very busy just now, thank you very much, good day. This was recorded, with no particular display of excitement, by an extremely attractive young woman who appeared to be in her late twenties, an artist from London who had missed but one summer at Loch Ness in seven years. She wore sandals, dungarees, a firmly stretched black pullover, and gold earrings. Her name was Mary Piercy, and her toes were painted pink. The bulletin board where she recorded the sighting resembled the kind used in railway stations for the listing of incoming trains.

The office walls were decorated with photographs of the monster in various postures – basking, cruising, diving, splashing, looking up inquisitively. A counter was covered with some of the essential bibliography: the bureau's annual report (twenty-nine sightings the previous year), J. A. Carruth's *Loch Ness and Its Monster* (The Abbey Press, Fort Augustus), Tim Dinsdale's *Loch Ness Monster* (Routledge & Kegan Paul, London), and a report by the Joint Air Reconnaissance Centre of the Royal Air Force on a motion picture of the monster swimming about half a mile on the lake's surface. These books and documents could, in turn, lead the interested reader to less available but nonetheless highly relevant works such as R.T. Gould's *The Loch Ness Monster and Others* and Constance Whyte's *More Than a Legend*.

My children looked over the photographs with absorption but not a great deal of awe, and they bought about a dozen postcards with glossy prints of a picture of the monster – three humps showing, much the same sight that the innkeeper had described – that had been taken by a man named Stuart, directly across the lake from Urquhart Castle. The three younger girls then ran out into the meadow and began to pick daisies and buttercups. Their mother and sister sat down in the sun to read about the creature in the lake, and to write postcards. We were on our way to Inverness, but with no need to hurry. 'Dear Grammy, we came to see the monster today.'

From the office to the camera-observation platform to the caravan that served as a pocket mess hall, I wandered around among the crew, was offered and accepted tea, and squinted with imaginary experience up and down the lake, where the whitecaps had, if anything, increased. Among the crew at the time were two

Canadians, a Swede, an Australian, three Americans, two Englishmen, a Welshman, and one Scot. Two were women. When I asked one of the crew members if he knew what some of the others did, vocationally, when they were not at Loch Ness, he said, 'I'm not sure what they are. We don't go into that.' This was obviously a place where now was all that mattered, and in such a milieu it is distinctly pleasant to accept that approach to things. Nonetheless, I found that I couldn't adhere completely to this principle, and I did find out that one man was a medical doctor, another a farmer, another a retired naval officer, and that several, inevitably, were students. The daily watch begins at four in the morning and goes on, as one fellow put it, 'as long as we can stand up.' It has been the pattern among the hundreds of sightings reported that the early-morning hours are the most promising ones. Camera stations are manned until ten at night, dawn and sunset being so close to midnight at that latitude in summer, but the sentries tend to thin out with the lengthening of the day. During the autumn the size of the crew reduces precipitously toward one.

One man lives at the headquarters all year long. His name is Clem Lister Skelton. 'I've been staring at that bloody piece of water since five o'clock,' he said, while he drank tea in the mess caravan.

'Is there a technique?' I asked him.

'Just look,' he said. 'Look. Run your eye over the water in one quick skim. What we're looking for is not hard to see. You just sit and sort of gaze at the loch, that's all. Mutter a few incantations. That's all there is to do. In wintertime, very often, it's just myself. And of course one keeps a very much more perfunctory watch in the winter. I saw it once in a snowstorm, though, and that was the only time I've had a clear view of the head and neck. The neck is obviously very mobile. The creature was quite big, but it wasn't as big as a seventy-foot MFV.

128

Motor fishing vessel. I'd been closer to it, but I hadn't seen as much of it before. I've seen it eight times. The last time was in September. Only the back. Just the sort of upturned boat, which is the classic view of it.'

Skelton drank some more tea and refilled a cup he had given me. 'I must know what it is,' he went on. 'I shall never rest peacefully until I know what it is. Some of the largest creatures in the world are out there, and we can't name them. It may take ten years, but we're going to identify the genus. Most people are not as fanatical as I, but I would like to see this through to the end, if I don't get too broke first.'

Skelton is a tall, offhand man, English, with reddish hair that is dishevelled in long strings from the thinning crown of his head. In outline, Skelton's life there in the caravan on the edge of the high meadow over the lake, in a place that must be uncorrectably gloomy during the wet rains of winter, seemed cagelike and hopeless to me – unacceptably lonely. The impression he gave was of a man who had drawn a circle around himself many hundreds of miles from the rest of his life. But how could I know? He was saying that he had flown Supermarine Spitfires for the RAF during the Second World War. His father had been a soldier, and when Skelton was a boy, he lived, as he put it, 'all over the place'. As an adult, he became first an actor, later a writer and director of films. He acted in London in plays like *March Hare* and *Saraband for Dead Lovers*. One film he directed was, in his words, 'a dreadful thing called *Saul and David*'. These appearances on the surface apparently did not occur so frequently that he needed to do nothing else for a livelihood. He also directed, in the course of many years, several hundred educational films. The publisher who distributed some of these films was David James, a friend of Skelton's, and at that time a Member of Parliament. James happened to be, as well, the founder of the

Loch Ness Phenomena Investigation Bureau – phenomena, because, for breeding purposes, there would have to be at least two monsters living in the lake at any one time, probably more, and in fact two had on occasion been sighted simultaneously. James asked Skelton if he would go up to the lake and give the bureau the benefit of his technical knowledge of movie cameras. 'Anything for a laugh,' Skelton had said to James. This was in the early nineteen-sixties. 'I came for a fortnight,' Skelton said now, in the caravan. 'And I saw it. I wanted to know what it was, and I've wanted to know what it was ever since. I thought I'd have time to write up here, but I haven't. I don't do anything now except hunt this beast.'

Skelton talked on about what the monster might be – a magnified newt, a long-necked variety of giant seal, an unextinct *Elasmosaurus*. Visitors wandered by in groups outside the caravan, and unexplained strangers kept coming in for tea. In the air was a feeling, utterly belied by the relative permanence of the place, of a country carnival on a two-night stand. The caravans themselves, in their alignment, suggested a section of a midway. I remembered a woman shouting to attract people to a big caravan on a carnival midway one night in May in New Jersey. That was some time ago. I must have been nineteen. The woman, who was standing on a small platform, was fifty or sixty, and she was trying to get people to go into the caravan to see big jungle cats, I suppose, and brown bears – 'Ferocious Beasts', at any rate, according to block lettering on the side of the caravan. A steel cage containing a small black bear had been set up on two sawhorses outside the caravan – a fragment to imply what might be found on a larger scale inside.

So young that it was no more than two feet from nose to tail, the bear was engaged in desperate motion, racing along one side of the cage from corner to corner, striking the steel bars bluntly with its nose. Whirling then, tossing

130

its head over its shoulder like a racing swimmer, it turned and bolted crazily for the opposite end. Its eyes were deep red, and shining in a kind of full-sighted blindness. It had gone mad there in the cage, and its motion, rhythmic and tortured, never ceased, back and forth, back and forth, the head tossing with each jarring turn. The animal abraded its flanks on the steel bars as it ran. Hair and skin had scraped from its sides so that pink flesh showed in the downpour of the carnival arc-lights. Blood drained freely through the thinned hair of its belly and dropped onto the floor of the cage. What had a paralysing effect on me was the animal's almost perfect and now involuntary rhythm – the wild toss of the head after the crash into the corner, the turn, the scraping run, the crash again at the other end, never stopping, metronomic – the exposed interior of some brutal and organic timepiece.

Beside the cage, the plump, impervious woman, red-faced, red-nosed, kept shouting to the crowds, but she said to me, leaning down, her own eyes bloodshot, 'Why don't you move on, sonny, if you ain't going to buy a ticket? Beat it. Come on, now. Move on.'

'We argue about what it is,' Skelton said. 'I'm inclined to think it's a giant slug, but there is an amazingly impressive theory for its being a worm. You can't rule out that it's one of the big dinosaurs, but I think this is more wishful thinking than anything else.' In the late nineteen-thirties, a large and exotic footprint was found along the shore of Loch Ness. It was meticulously studied by various people and was assumed, for a time, to be an impression from a foot or flipper of the monster. Eventually, the print was identified. Someone who owned the preserved foot of a hippopotamus had successfully brought off a hoax that put layers of mockery and incredibility over the creature in the lake for many years. The Second World War further diverted any serious interest that amateurs or naturalists might have taken. Sightings continued, however, in a consistent pattern, and finally, in the early nineteen-sixties, the Loch Ness Phenomena Investigation Bureau was established. 'I have no plans whatever for leaving,' Skelton said. 'I am prepared to stay here ad infinitum. All my worldly goods are here.'

A dark-haired young woman had stepped into the caravan and poured herself a cup of tea. Skelton, introducing her to me, said, 'If the beast has done nothing else, it has brought me a wife. She was studying Gaelic and Scottish history at Edinburgh University, and she walked into the glen one day, and I said, "That is the girl I am going to marry." ' He gestured toward a window of the caravan, which framed a view of the hills and the lake. 'The Great Glen is one of the most beautiful places in the world,' he continued. 'It is peaceful here. I'd be happy here all my life, even if there were nothing in the loch. I've even committed the unforgivable sin of going to sleep in the sun during a flat calm. With enough time, we could shoot the beast with a crossbow and a line, and get a bit of skin. We could also shoot a small transmitter into its hide and learn more than we know now about its habits and characteristics.'

The creature swims with remarkable speed, as much as ten or fifteen knots when it is really moving. It makes no noise other than seismic splashes, but it is apparently responsive in a highly sensitive way to sound. A shout, an approaching engine, any loud report, will send it into an immediate dive, and this shyness is in large part the cause of its inaccessibility, and therefore of its mystery. Curiously, though, reverberate sound was what apparently brought the creature widespread attention, for the first sequence of frequent sightings occurred in

1933 when the A-82 was blasted into the cliffsides of the western shore of the lake. Immense boulders kept falling into the depths, and shock waves from dynamite repeatedly ran through the water, causing the creature to lose confidence in its environment and to alter, at least temporarily, its shy and preferentially nocturnal life. In that year it was first observed on land, perhaps attempting to seek a way out forever from the detonations that had alarmed it. A couple named Spicer saw it, near Inverarigaig, and later described its long, serpentine neck, followed by an ungainly hulk of body, lurching toward the lake and disappearing into high undergrowth as they approached.

With the exception of one report recorded in the sixth century, which said that a monster (fitting the description of the contemporary creatures in the lake) had killed a man with a single bite, there have been no other examples of savagery on its part. To the contrary, its sensitivity to people seems to be acute, and it keeps a wide margin between itself and mankind. In all likelihood, it feeds on fish and particularly on eels, of which there are millions in the lake. Loch Ness is unparalleled in eel-fishing circles, and has drawn commercial eel fishermen from all over the United Kingdom. The monster has been observed with its neck bent down in the water, like a swan feeding. When the creatures die, they apparently settle into the seven-hundred-foot floor of the lake, where the temperature is always forty-two degrees Fahrenheit – so cold that the lake is known for never giving up its dead. Loch Ness never freezes, despite its high latitude, so if the creature breathes air, as has seemed apparent from the reports of observers who have watched its mouth rhythmically opening and closing, it does not lose access to the surface in winter. It clearly prefers the smooth, sunbaked waterscapes of summer, however, for it seems to love to bask in the sun, like an upturned boat, slowly rolling, plunging, squirming around with what can only be taken as pleasure. By observers' reports, the creature has two pairs of lateral flippers, and when it swims off, tail thrashing, it leaves behind it a wake as impressive as the wake of a small warship. When it dives from a still position, it inexplicably goes down without leaving a bubble. When it dives as it swims, it leaves on the surface a churning signature of foam.

Skelton leaned back against the wall of the caravan in a slouched and nonchalant posture. He was wearing a dark blue tie that was monogrammed in small block letters sewn with white thread – LNI (Loch Ness Investigation). Above the monogram and embroidered also in white thread was a small depiction of the monster – humps undulant, head high, tail extending astern. Skelton gave the tie a flick with one hand. 'You get this with a five-pound membership,' he said.

The sea-serpent effect given by the white thread on the tie was less a stylization than an attempt toward a naturalistic sketch. As I studied it there, framed on Skelton's chest, the thought occurred to me that there was something inconvenient about the monster's actual appearance. In every sense except possibly the sense that involves cruelty, the creature in Loch Ness is indeed a monster. An average taken from many films and sightings gives its mature length at about forty feet. Its general appearance is repulsive, in the instant and radical sense in which reptiles are repulsive to many human beings, and any number of people might find difficulty in accepting a creature that looks like the one that was slain by St George. Its neck, about six feet long, columnar, powerfully muscled, is the neck of a serpent. Its head, scarcely broader than the neck, is a serpent's head, with uncompromising, lenticular eyes. Sometimes as it swims it holds its head and neck erect. The creature's mouth is at least a foot wide. Its body undulates. Its skin glistens when wet and appears coarse, mottled, grey and elephantine when exposed to the air long enough to become dry. The tail, long and columnar, stretches back to something of a point. It seemed to me, sitting there at Headquarters, that the classical, mythical, dragon likeness of this animate thing – the modified dinosaur, the fantastically exaggerated newt – was an impediment to the work of the investigation bureau, which has no pertinent interest in what the monster resembles or calls to mind but a great deal in what it actually is, the goal being a final and positive identification of the genus.

'What we need is a good, lengthy, basking sighting,' Skelton said. 'We've had one long surfacing – twenty-five minutes. I saw it. Opposite Urquhart Castle. We only had a twelve-inch lens then, at four and a half miles. We have thirty-six-inch lenses now. We need a long, clear, close-up – in colour.'

My children had watched, some months earlier, the killing of a small snake on a lawn in Maryland. About eighteen inches long, it came out from a basement-window well, through a covering lattice of redwood, and was noticed with shouts and shrieks by the children and a young retriever that barked at the snake and leaped about it in a circle. We were the weekend guests of another family, and eight children in all crowded around the snake, which had been gliding slowly across the lawn during the moments after it had been seen, but had now stopped and was turning its head from side to side in apparent indecision. Our host hurried into his garage and came running back to the lawn with a long shovel. Before he killed the snake, his wife urged him not to. She said the snake could not possibly be poisonous. He said, 'How do you know?' The children, mine and theirs, looked back and forth from him to her. The dog began to bark more rapidly and at a higher pitch.

'It has none of the markings. There is nothing tri-angular about its head,' she told him.

'That may very well be,' he said. 'But you can't be sure.'

'It is *not* poisonous. Leave it alone. Look at all these children.'

'I can't help that.'

'It is *not* poisonous.'

'How do you know?'

'I know.'

He hit the snake with the flat of the shovel, and it writhed. He hit it again. It kept moving. He hit it a third time, and it stopped. Its underside, whitish green, seg-mental, turned up. The children moved in for a closer look.

From Birnam Wood to Dunsinane

In most families, a generation or two is time enough to erase even a major infamy, but centuries upon centuries have not in this respect been kind to the Macbeths, as anyone knows who knows one. I've known several Macbeths, and I particularly remember the moments in which I met them, because in most instances a faint shadow seemed to cross their faces when their surname was exposed to yet another stranger. The latest of these is R. G. Macbeth, of Scarsdale. We were introduced – as travellers, as strangers, in a small town in New England – by a motel-keeper who was serving our breakfast and who in her friendly way seemed to think that we would have much to say to each other simply because our names were derivationally Scottish. This Macbeth was a big, broad-shouldered man with bright eyes and an engagingly unprepossessing manner. As it happened, he did have a lot to say. He had scarcely sat down before he was well into a mild harangue about the injuries that had been done to his family through poetic licence and dramatic journalism – manipulations of the pen. He said that his collateral ancestor Macbeth, King of Scotland, was a good king and is buried with other Scottish kings on the island Iona in a sanctuary where only authentic and duly entitled kings are at rest; that no one who had poached the throne of Scotland would ever have been buried, or at least would have long remained buried, on Iona; that Macbeth, in 1040, killed King Duncan not in bed but in battle; that Macbeth's claim to rule the Scots was as legitimate as Duncan's, each, through his mother, being a great-grandson of King Kenneth I; and that Macbeth settled the claim, as was the custom in his time, with his sword in fair and open fight. His reign lasted seventeen years. I could be well assured that something quite different from tyranny or depravity was the atmosphere that generally emanated from his fortress on the summit of Dunsinane Hill.

I said to Mr Macbeth, 'I'm sorry you have this cross to bear.'

Macbeth lifted his coffee cup, indicating that he would drink to that. He drank. Then he said, 'I've never been to Scotland. In a year or two, though, I'm going to go.'

I said, 'Let me give you a name and address. Donald Sinclair, Balbeggie, Perthshire. I'll write it down. He's a farmer. He's the cousin of a friend of mine. I don't know Sinclair very well, but I don't think he would mind if you were to seek him out, which is what I did once. I was in Scotland with my family, and one day – just for the experience – we went by the most direct way we could find from Birnam Wood to Dunsinane. It's a ten-mile trip. Sinclair calls himself a tenant farmer. Technically, that's what he is, but his father-in-law happens to be his landlord, and the family owns a very handsome piece of Perthshire – five thousand acres. Their estate is called Dunsinnan, and more or less in the middle of it is Dunsinane Hill.'

Macbeth slowly set down his plastic coffee cup on the Formica surface of the table. I told him the details of the pilgrimage as I had made it.

Birnam Wood, on the edge of the Craigvinean Forest, stands across the River Tay from a medieval town, Dunkeld, and has been replaced to some extent by Birnam, a village that developed in the late nineteenth century. Birnam Wood now is deep and thick, dark green, with an understory of gorse and bracken and white slashes of birch angling upward among larches and pines. In all likelihood, the boughs of such trees could not have been the boughs that went to Dunsinane. Apparently the forest was once predominantly oak. The present Birnam Wood, cut who knows how many times, seems to be merely a collateral descendant of the forest that once was there, for the presence of a number of slim oaks among the pines suggests what must have been, in the virgin stand, the climax tree. The army assembled by Siward, Malcolm, and Macduff would have marched under oak leaves. By the river is one immensely impressive piece of evidence suggesting that this was so. One tree, an oak, remains from – according to local testimony – the time of Macbeth. It stands in a riparian grove of grasses, weeds, and rusting junk. Nothing much is made of it. I used up half a morning finding it. A postman on the principal street of Birnam had told me about it. 'The old trees are away now, unfortunately. But there is still one left. It is propped up.' We picked our way downhill – my four small daughters, my wife, and I – along dirt pathways strewn with discarded plastic bottles and fragments of broken glass. The groundscape was somewhat cleaner and more inviting closer to the river, where another path ran along parallel to the current and passed under the high canopies of trees at least a century old. These were whips, seedlings, saplings by comparison with the tree we finally found. There it was, standing without fence or fanfare, its trunk outmassing the Heidelberg tun, its roemerian canopy all but stopping the sunlight: the last tree of Birnam Wood, a living monument to the value of staying put.

My wife and children and I joined hands, and we

wrapped ourselves to the tree with arms extended. The six of us reached less than halfway around. The big oak was so gnarled that it appeared to be covered with highly magnified warts. Each of ten principal limbs had the diameter of a major oak in itself, and the lower ones, jutting out almost horizontally, were supported in six places by columns set in the ground. One great limb was dead. In the base of the trunk were cavelike holes. Lichen grew on the bark as if the tree were already down and mouldering. But despite all that, the tree was green throughout its canopy – leafy and alive. This big oak alone could have camouflaged an army.

We sat down on the riverbank and had lunch. The Tay was fast, clear, and shallow, and about two hundred yards downstream was a small rip, a touch of white water. The flow was southerly, in the general direction of Dunsinane, so the army would have moved for some distance along the river on its way to the hill. We ate cold roast beef, white chocolate, and Islay Mini-Dunlop cheese. I reached up and took a leaf from the great oak, and we began the journey.

First, we stopped in at the Esso Autodiesel & Petrol Agency in Birnam and had the tank of our car filled, for five shillings sixpence halfpenny the gallon. The attendant gave the children Esso tiger tails. Below Birnam the riverine countryside was lush with wheat fields, haycocks, oats, barley. Multicoloured lupins and wild foxgloves grew in meadows where herds of Aberdeen Angus were sleeping, all draped together with their necks across the necks of the cows beside them. It was a clear day, warm but not hot. A tractor ploughing a field was followed by flights of seagulls. The gulls were eating the worms that the tractor turned up. We moved through a grove of seventy-foot cedars, copper beeches, and hemlocks on a dark lane running among standing stones, through weirdly overgrown formal gardens, and past an Italianate castle no more than a century old, now boarded shut and falling to ruin. We later found in a book on Dunkeld and Birnam that this (Murthly Castle) had been the home of an exotic peer who had once ornamented the grounds with herds of buffalo from Wyoming. In his milieu, he may not have been eccentric. Even today, we know someone in the same part of Perthshire who keeps a considerable herd of pet red deer, and when he goes off in summer to the far north – to Caithness – he takes his red deer with him in chartered freight cars.

Murthly Hospital, for mental patients, came soon after Murthly Castle and was about a third of the way from Birnam Wood to Dunsinane. Like the decaying structure upriver, the main buildings of the hospital, amorphous and ugly, must have been about a century old, and in their setting among woods and fields by the Tay they did not seem as forbidding in the sunlight as they must in the gloom of rain. The place belied itself, if it ever could, this day. Women sat on benches in brightly coloured straw hats. Men in coveralls bowled on a lawn. Others gardened. Distress was invisible, but nonetheless my children were unnaturally quiet. Doctors crossed the grounds in white jackets. A big nurse, whose size was a kind of manifesto of control, carried a fragile and extremely old woman in her arms. Rows of stone cottages had names over their doors like Tuke, Robertson, Bruce. Among them, a giant and rusting television aerial was planted in the earth like a tree. One of the men on the bowling court left the game and ran toward us, smiling and waving his arms. I did not for a moment know what I wanted to do. He was running hard. Was I going to avoid him and renew, in one more way, his hurt; or was I going to become enskeined in a dialogue that could, in the end, be even less successful in the breaking? I left him behind, standing by the road, without expression, watching us go.

The country opened out again beyond the hospital, and the river made an erratic series of turns to the north, the east, the south-east, and, finally, the south-west, forming an irregular loop about two miles broad. Anybody moving overland from Birnam Wood to Dunsinane would cross this loop, and so did we, first going through the Haugh of Kercock, a low-lying meadow by the river. In a fank in the meadow, men were shearing sheep. Lambs were bleating wildly. Shorn ewes stood around looking silly and naked. One man had the head of a ewe in his arms, and was wrestling with her desperately, rolling on the ground. Moving on, we skirted a marshland called the Bloody Inches. Beautiful farm country followed toward Kinclaven, a village by the Tay, on the far side of the loop. In the fields, huge strawstacks had been constructed like houses – rectangular, with vertical walls, and tops sloping up to ridge-lines. Moving along an unpaved lane, we came to a church that was black with age, and among the tombstones beside it a man was digging a grave. We stopped to ask him the way to Dunsinane. He said he had been digging graves there forty-four years and had been born and raised in Kinclaven but had no idea how to get to Dunsinane. He said, 'It's not far. It's a small place, I can tell you that.' His shovel struck something in the ground. He explained that when he digs graves he often encounters the foundations of churches that, one after another, had been on the site before this one. A church must have been there when Macbeth's castle stood on Dunsinane Hill. According to the Scottish historian R. L. Mackie, Macbeth was so religious that he once made a pilgrimage to Rome. All the way to the Vatican and back, he flung money at the poor. Since he lived less than five miles away from Kinclaven, he and Lady Macbeth must have gone to church here from time to time.

We crossed the river, made a right, went through a

railway embankment, made a left at Cargill Smithy, and began a long upgrade toward Gallowhill, Wolfhill, and Dunsinnan, through villages of strawstacks, and more wheat, oats, and barley in dark red earth. We found Donald Sinclair among his steadings, some two miles from Dunsinane Hill.

Sinclair seemed amused that we wanted to climb his hill, and not at all put out. I had thought that people must come in battalions to Dunsinane, and that Sinclair probably spent a lot of his time protecting his land. He said that was not the case. A busload of Boy Scouts from Perth might turn up once in a rare while, but that was about all. Few people seem to realize that there really is a Dunsinane Hill. Shakespeare, he said, took an 'n' out of Dunsinnan and added an 'e', but did not create the hill. 'The name in Gaelic means "hill of the ants". Streams of little men went up and down the hill when the castle was being built. Shall we go?'

We drove with him through fields and in woodland, made a few turns, and all at once saw a high green hill fringed with rowan trees and mountain ash in blossom. Dunsinane is at the south-western end of the serrated line of the Sidlaw Hills. The other Sidlaws, reaching away to the north-east, were all mauve-brown with heather, and Dunsinane stood out among them because it was bright green. Heather apparently will not grow where man has ever performed his constructions. Even from the foot of Dunsinane, we could see that its summit was flat – absolutely truncated, as if it had been sliced level with a knife. We started up its grassy, southern slope. Sinclair's Herefords were grazing there. 'I raise beef cattle,' he said. 'They summer on the hill. When a busload of Boy Scouts comes, it is much to my horror, because I've got a bull amongst the cows here.' Sinclair was wearing wide-wale corduroy trousers, a threadbare baggy sweater, a shirt, a wool tie. Still in his forties, a tall man, he looked weathered, as if he had always been there. He seemed to be at one with his land and his hill, and nothing about his loose-postured walk suggested that he was a graduate of Sandhurst, which he was – a career military man, born on a wheat farm in Manitoba, raised in England, an army officer from the Second World War until the early nineteen-sixties, when he became the tenant farmer of Dunsinane Hill. We went around a shoulder of the terrain. 'There he is,' Sinclair said. We passed close by a congenial-looking Hereford bull. He was rust-red, almost top-heavy, the kind of animal that appears to consist of about nine tons of solid steak, and, with his white-rug face, to be as fierce as Ferdinand. 'We call him Old Joe.'

The slopes of the hill rose and converged with an almost volcanic symmetry, so the climb became quite steep. We passed a spring. 'This is where Macbeth got his water,' Sinclair said. 'The sort of outer fortifications must have reached this far.' We kept moving up, breathing hard and not talking for a while, until Sinclair paused for a moment, tilted his head back, looked up at the summit, and said, 'It's pretty impregnable, I should think. I shouldn't like to climb up here and have people pouring boiling oil on me.'

The summit was flat and oval, and Macbeth's floor plan was evident there, for the foundation protruded in lumpy ridges under the turf. The castle was no cramped little broch. It was a hundred and twenty feet wide and two hundred and twenty-five feet long – just slightly larger than the Parthenon. Hill of the ants, indeed: Macbeth apparently did not do things by halves. The view from the summit over the patchwork Scottish countryside was extraordinary. It is a virtual certainty that Shakespeare never set eyes on Dunsinane. If he had, he would have described it. In fact, his entire description of Dunsinane Hill comes in two words, 'high' and 'great'.

Macbeth shall never vanquished be until
Great Birnam Wood to high Dunsinane Hill
Shall come against him.

Great Dunsinane he strongly fortifies:
Some say he's mad.

Curlews and oyster catchers cried overhead. This was
June, and we could see the Grampians, far in the distance,
with snow still on them. We could see, three hundred
and sixty degrees around us, a fifth of Scotland – to Fife,
to Dundee – and out over the North Sea. It would be
hard to imagine a more apt or beautiful setting for a
fortress home. Sinclair said that the Picts had chosen the
spot centuries before Macbeth, and that Dunsinane had
been only one of a whole line of Pictish forts in the
Sidlaws – 'a sort of defence effort against the Vikings.'
We sat down on the base of a rampart. A cool, erratic
wind was blowing. Sinclair told us, offhandedly, that the
supposed Stone of Scone now in Westminster Abbey is
actually a worthless rock from Dunsinane Hill. He said
that the real Stone of Scone had been buried in Dunsinane Hill long ago, when the substitute was chosen,
and that the real one had been dug up in the nineteenth
century only to be reburied after a short time, and that
despite all the more recent flurries about the (fake)
Stone of Scone in Westminster Abbey, the real one was
still there in the hill. Sinclair pointed out Scone, over
toward Perth, and added that that was the dullest direction to look in, for, with the dubious exceptions of Scone
and Perth, 'you can't see anything madly exciting'.
Closer in and on a more northerly line, he called attention to a small stone house trimmed in red, and he said,
'That is where Macbeth settled his three wise women.'
Moving his hand, pointing, he said, 'That farm down
there is called Balmalcolm. The next one is Fairy Green,
where they found a Pictish stone called the Spunky Dell.

The trees down here on the north slope were planted by my father-in-law. He's reforesting. They are five-year-old Scotch pines and some larch.'

Macbeth did not die at Dunsinane. Birnam Wood moved, and so forth, according to Holinshed's questionable Chronicles, but Macbeth was ignominiously driven away, a fugitive king humbled before his people, and he lived three more years before he was killed, by Malcolm Canmore (Big-Headed Malcolm), on some undramatic moor in Aberdeen. I had been reading W. C. Mackenzie's history of the Highlands only a few days before this, and there on the summit of Dunsinane I found that I could almost remember verbatim Mackenzie's summary line: 'By the irony of circumstances, Macbeth, branded as long as literature lasts with the stain of blood, was the friend of the poor, the protector of the monks, and the first Scottish king whose name appears in ecclesiastical records as the benefactor of the Church.' It simply was not in him to shout at an enemy here on these ramparts in the hour of his death:

> I will not yield,
> To kiss the ground before young Malcolm's feet
> And to be baited with the rabble's curse.
> Though Birnam Wood be come to Dunsinane,
> And thou oppos'd, being of no woman born,
> Yet I will try the last. Before my body
> I throw my warlike shield. Lay on, Macduff,
> And damn'd be him that first cries 'Hold, enough!'

The race being what it is, we prefer him the second way, and Shakespeare knew what we wanted. I had been twirling by its stem the leaf from the Birnam oak, and I dropped it on the top of the hill. We went down to Sinclair's farmhouse for tea, and tea included, among other things, banana sandwiches and Nesquik chocolate milk shakes.

Mr Macbeth, after a struggle over the check, paid for my breakfast. As we parted, he told me that he had once been a salesman of advertising space for a magazine, and that he had spent half his days in reception foyers waiting to get in to see various kinds of executives. On arrival, he would give his name routinely to the receptionist, then sit down, pick up a magazine, and wait. During this interval, slow, obscure, primordial stirrings would apparently go on in the receptionist's mind, for time and again – and never, he thought, with conscious intent – the receptionist would eventually say to him, 'You may go in now, Mr Macduff.'